"This compelling reflection on Isaiah's extraordinary portrait of the Servant has a simplicity and directness which will provoke surprise, gratitude and worship. Pastoral and devotional in tone, it illuminates these remarkable chapters through thought-provoking illustration and application that will warm the heart, strengthen faith and encourage mission. A wonderful resource for spiritual renewal!"

JONATHAN LAMB, Minister-at-large, Keswick Ministries; IFES Vice-President; Former Director of Langham Preaching

"*The Beauty of the Cross* is a wonderful resource for meaningful reflection on our Lord's finished work at Calvary. Tim Chester does a fine job of focusing on rich texts in Isaiah 52 – 53, and then leads the reader to pray, meditate and praise our great God for his perfect plan of redemption. Poignant quotes from church fathers and others, as well as personal illustrations, are value added to this well-organized devotional. It's a treasure! *The Beauty of the Cross* will be a great addition to any believer's library."

MARY K. MOHLER, Author, *Growing in Gratitude*

"This is a book to savour! Tim Chester has done an exquisite job in walking us gently through the richness of Isaiah's vision of Jesus Christ, the Servant of the Lord, as he walks to (and through) his death in our place. Beautifully paced, theologically rich and deeply rooted in the real world—take it, read it slowly, and drink in its Christ-saturated truth!"

GARY MILLAR, Principal, Queensland Theological College

"Tim brings readers right into the bright light of Lent—Christ the Lord. Like the old hymn, Chester's meditations and expositions from Isaiah invite you to turn your eyes upon Jesus, to look fully at the face of the suffering Servant, and to see how the things of earth grow dim in the divine wattage of Christ's glory and grace."

JEFF MEDDERS, Lead Pastor, Redeemer Church, Tomball, Texas; Author, *Humble Calvinism* and *Rooted*

"Here is a book to treasure and to share. Tim leads us on a journey through some of the Bible's most precious chapters, for a rediscovery of the Christ who has walked our road, and who goes with us still. *The Beauty of the Cross* will be a rich blessing to you."

LEWIS ALLEN, Senior Pastor, Hope Church, Huddersfield, UK; Director, Gospel Yorkshire

"The cross of Jesus is the centre of the Christian faith. None of us thrive when we drift far from the foot of the cross. It is there that we discover that God is not as the world thinks he is; that our only hope does not lie in ourselves; and that the hideous instrument of torture, the cross, is actually profoundly beautiful. Tim Chester's book, *The Beauty of the Cross*, will be a great companion and guide as you meditate on the cross of Jesus."

PETER MEAD, Director, Cor Deo; Author, *Lost in Wonder*

TIM CHESTER

The Beauty of the Cross

Reflections for Lent from
Isaiah 52 and 53

The Beauty of the Cross
© Tim Chester/The Good Book Company, 2019

Published by:
The Good Book Company

Tel (UK): 0333 123 0880
Tel (US): 866 244 2165
Email (UK): info@thegoodbook.co.uk
Email (US): info@thegoodbook.com

Websites:
UK: www.thegoodbook.co.uk
North America: www.thegoodbook.com
Australia: www.thegoodbook.com.au
New Zealand: www.thegoodbook.co.nz

thegoodbook
COMPANY

ISBN: 9781784983710 | Printed in the UK

Design by André Parker

CONTENTS

INTRODUCTION

On holy ground

"Take off your sandals, for the place where you are standing is holy ground." This is what Moses is told when he encounters God at the burning bush (Exodus 3 v 5).

Writing about Isaiah 52 – 53 has felt like standing on holy ground. Though he wrote 800 years before Jesus came, Isaiah gives us such a rich and intimate portrait of the death and resurrection of Jesus.

Here, as clearly as almost anywhere else in the Bible, we see the true meaning of what was taking place as Jesus was nailed to the cross.

But this section of Isaiah is not simply an explanation. It's a powerful and affecting portrait of the personal cost of our salvation. Here we see the man of sorrows, disfigured beyond recognition and yet also satisfied with what his suffering achieves.

This is hallowed ground. And God invites us to take off our shoes, as it were, and look at Jesus. "See, my servant," he says in Isaiah 52 v 13.

My prayer for this book has been, "Hallowed be your name". I want us to say as we explore these verses together, "Wow, that's amazing!" Not in a light-hearted way. I want our jaws to drop as we stand open-mouthed before the cross, lost for words as we see the love of Christ in all its fullness.

Some of these readings will then give suggestions for how this applies to our daily lives. But sometimes it's enough simply to have our view of Christ widened—for how we worship is always the catalyst for how we live.

And if these reflections on the cross leave you wanting to sing your praises aloud, you'll find a song based on Isaiah 52 – 53 on page 158.

We often speak or sing about the cross. Of course we do; it's central to our faith. This section of Isaiah is an invitation to pause; to take it slow; to go down deep...

THE BEGINNING OF LENT

*The
Servant*

ASH WEDNESDAY

Acts 8 v 26-39

Come with me to a desert road. The hardened earth stretches away towards the horizon, where it dissolves into the shimmer of the heat. Along the edge of the road walks a man—a man named Philip. Behind him a cloud of dust is slowly approaching, out of which emerges a chariot. Philip runs towards it and starts jogging alongside. In the chariot is a man. We can tell immediately he's a man of importance—a politician perhaps. He's reading an ancient text, the story of a mysterious servant of God, but his face betrays his confusion. Between breaths Philip shouts up, "Do you understand what you're reading?" "How can I," the man replies, "unless someone explains it to me?" (Acts 8 v 30-31)

The man in the chariot, an official in the court of the queen of Ethiopia, is not the first person, nor the last, to wonder who the servant is.

The prophet Isaiah has four songs about the servant of the LORD in chapters 42, 49, 50 and 52 – 53. Sometimes the servant appears to be the nation of Israel. "You are my servant, Israel," says 49 v 3, "in whom

I will display my splendour". Yet two verses later, the servant is someone other than Israel—someone who will *redeem* Israel (49 v 5).

The nation of Israel was supposed to display God's splendour to the nations, to be a light to the nations, to attract the world to God's ways. But more often than not, Israel was drawn away from God and towards the ways of the nations. As a result, they brought God's name into disrepute. The consequence was exile.

Isaiah lived 200 years before the exile. But he looked ahead to the day when God's people would be defeated by the Babylonians and dragged off to Babylon. In these songs he speaks words of comfort to those in captivity (40 v 1). He promises that King Cyrus, the king of the Persians, will defeat the Babylonians and let God's people return home. So in one sense, King Cyrus is God's servant (44 v 28; 45 v 1-7). Isaiah even calls Cyrus—a foreign king who never acknowledged God—God's "anointed", his messiah, his christ (45 v 1). Whether Cyrus recognises it or not, God has chosen him to deliver God's people and bring them home.

But the exile in Babylon was a pointer to a greater exile, and the rescue from Babylon was a pointer to a greater rescue. The prophets warned the surrounding nations not to rejoice in Israel's defeat because it was (and still is) a sign of God's judgment against all humanity. Adam and Eve were expelled from the Garden of Eden with an angel brandishing a flaming sword to prevent their return to the place where they had once walked with God (Genesis 3 v 8, 23-24). Ever since, humanity has lived in exile from God. "We all, like sheep, have gone astray," says Isaiah 53 v 6.

So even when the Israelites eventually returned to their homeland, they still felt like slaves for they were stilled ruled by foreign kings (Nehemiah 9 v 36-37). Nor had their return solved the underlying problems—their sin and God's judgment. That required a greater rescue and a greater Servant.

The Ethiopian eunuch reads from Isaiah's final servant song in Isaiah 53. "Tell me, please," he asks, "who is the prophet talking about, himself or someone else?" Philip is in no doubt who the ultimate Servant is. "Then Philip began with that very passage of Scripture," says Acts 8 v 35, "and told him the good news about Jesus". Isaiah points way beyond King Cyrus to King Jesus himself.

Isaiah's first servant song begins, "Here is my servant" (Isaiah 42 v 1). It's literally, "See, my servant". The final song begins with exactly the same words (Isaiah 52 v 13). This song cycle is an invitation to look at Jesus. We'll look at the first three songs over the coming three days. After that we'll slow down and take our time as we meditate on the fourth and greatest song in Isaiah 52 – 53. It's an opportunity to pause at the foot of the cross and look at Jesus.

Ash Wednesday is traditionally a day for confession and repentance. So let's begin by confessing that we have strayed like sheep, and let's come home in repentance to God. Let's pray that Isaiah would lead us to see Jesus the Servant afresh this Lent.

Meditate

Almighty and most merciful Father,
we have erred, and strayed from thy ways like lost sheep.

We have followed too much the devices and desires
of our own hearts.
We have offended against thy holy laws.
We have left undone those things
which we ought to have done;
and we have done those things
which we ought not to have done;
and there is no health in us.

But thou, O Lord, have mercy upon us,
miserable offenders.
Spare thou them, O God, which confess their faults.
Restore thou them that are penitent;
according to thy promises declared unto mankind
in Christ Jesus our Lord.

And grant, O most merciful Father, for his sake,
that we may hereafter live
a godly, righteous, and sober life,
to the glory of thy holy name. Amen.

The Book of Common Prayer
(based in part on Isaiah 53 v 6)

THURSDAY

Isaiah 42 v 1-7

A re you fighting fit and ready to do battle for the sake of Christ? Are you on fire for God today? There are times when Christians feel like this. But more often we feel a bit battered and bruised. We're not marching bravely into battle. We're more like wounded soldiers, limping along in trepidation.

If that's how you feel today, then Jesus is for you.

Three times we're told that Jesus the Servant will bring justice to the nations:

- *He will bring justice to the nations (v 1).*
- *He will bring forth justice (v 3).*
- *He establishes justice on earth (v 4).*

Justice here is not just the rule of law. The term describes the divine ordering of creation. So the servant's task is massive: he's going to re-establish God's righteous rule over the world.

But Jesus the Servant is not going to steam-roll God's kingdom into existence. Yes, he's a mighty King who "will not falter or be discouraged till he establishes justice on earth". Yet at the same time, he's gentle with wounded saints. Yes, he will crush evil. Yet at the same time, he tenderly cares for fragile souls.

He will not shout or cry out,
   or raise his voice in the streets.
A bruised reed he will not break,
   and a smouldering wick he will not snuff out.
                                              (Isaiah 42 v 2-3)

We have an open fire in our front room. Normally my wife, our family's resident pyromaniac, is the one who takes charge of it. But occasionally it falls to me to get it going. It always feels as if it has to be nurtured into life. Paper and kindling are lit first. Then larger pieces of wood can gradually be added. But if I'm not paying attention, then all too quickly the fire goes out, leaving the wood spluttering and smoking. With a bit of luck, though, gently blowing will fan it into flames again.

This is how Jesus nurtures weak and wounded Christians. He gradually builds us up. He doesn't give up on us when we splutter and smoke. Gently he blows the breath of his Spirit into our hearts.

In verses 5-7 God turns from talking *about* the servant to talk *to* the servant. The God who created the world is about to recreate it. Just as at creation God spoke and light replaced darkness (Genesis 1 v 2-3), so again light will dawn to liberate those in the bondage of spiritual darkness (Isaiah 42 v 6-7, 18-20). So it's perhaps no surprise to notice that the sword by which he conquers the nations is not made of cold steel. Instead his kingdom advances through "his teaching" (v 4)—through "the sword of the Spirit, which is the word of God" (Ephesians 6 v 17).

Think how easily we get frustrated with other people and how easily a sharp word can crush them. "People, for a little smoke, will quench the light," says the Puritan Richard Sibbes. "But we always see Christ cherishing even the smallest beginnings of a flame." He goes on to give this advice:

> *It is not wrong to hide the deficiencies of young Christians, excuse some of their failings, commend their achievements, cherish their progress, remove obstacles from their way, help them in every way to bear the yoke of religion with greater ease, to bring them to love God and his service, lest they have distaste for it before they know it … It would be good if, among Christians, one would work hard to give no offence while the other would work hard to take none.*

Meditate
Jesus said,
"The Spirit of the Sovereign LORD is on me,
because the LORD has anointed me
to proclaim good news to the poor.
He has sent me to bind up the broken-hearted,
to proclaim freedom for the captives
and release from darkness for the prisoners,
to proclaim the year of the LORD's favour."

Isaiah 61 v 1-2 and Luke 4 v 18-19

FRIDAY
Isaiah 49 v 1-6

What's it worth? You ask someone for a favour and they reply, "What's it worth?" In these verses we discover what the cross of Jesus is worth.

Israel had failed to be a light to the nations, but Jesus the Servant succeeds (John 8 v 12). What makes Jesus different? "You are my servant, Israel, in whom I will display my splendour" (Isaiah 49 v 3). It's in Jesus that we see the true holiness, grace, wisdom, justice, compassion, power and love of God. And what we see is splendid! For he displays God's splendour.

But what's he worth? "What is due to me is in the LORD's hand, and my reward is with my God" (v 4). God is going to reward the obedience of Jesus.

And what is that reward? His people Israel, yes. *But* that is not enough. The cross of Christ is worth more. The LORD says, "It is too small a thing for you to be my servant to restore the tribes of Jacob and bring back those of Israel I have kept" (v 6). *Too small a thing.* The cross deserves more. The cross achieves more. And so God says, "I will *also* make you a light for the Gentiles [non-Jews], that my salvation may reach to the ends of the earth".

Jesus left the glory of heaven. He did not cling to the rights of his divinity. He took on human form. He became, says Philippians 2 v 5-8, a servant, *the* Servant. He was obedient to death, even death on a cross. He was betrayed by a follower, abandoned by his friends, beaten, mocked, spat upon and crucified. He died under the darkness of judgment, forsaken by his Father.

What is that worth? It's worth the nations! Not one nation. Not two or three nations. People from the ends of the earth. Jesus deserves the praise of *every* nation. That's why we share the good news about Jesus with all the nations—because this is what the cross deserves.

In Isaiah 49 v 4 the Servant says, "What is due to me is in the LORD's hand". It's the language of the law court. It's literally "My judgment is in the LORD's hand". On earth, Jesus was tried by humanity and found guilty, condemned as a blasphemer and executed as a rebel. But that decision has been gloriously overturned in the court of heaven.

The account of the ascension of Jesus in Acts 1 draws on the vision in Daniel 7 where what Daniel sees is a courtroom. In that vision, Daniel sees Jesus (referred to as "a son of man") ascending through the clouds to be vindicated by the Ancient of Days. What does he receive from the Ancient of Days? The nations. "He was given authority, glory and sovereign power; all nations and peoples of every language worshipped him" (Daniel 7 v 14). Jesus echoes these words in the Great Commission: "All authority in heaven and on earth has been given to me. Therefore go and make disciples of all nations" (Matthew 28 v 18-19). Why do we go out in mission? To gather the nations to worship Jesus.

Every step we make in mission is a step towards the moment when people from every nation, tribe, language and tongue join together to cry, "Worthy is the Lamb, who was slain, to receive power and wealth and wisdom and strength and honour and glory and praise!" (Revelation 5 v 12).

It is *too small a thing* to be concerned just for your family or just your parish. Christ is worth more than that. How will you show this in the way you use your time, in the places you give your money to, and in the focus of your prayers? The cross of Christ deserves the nations.

Meditate

I cannot tell how silently he suffered,
As with his peace he graced this place of tears,
Or how his heart upon the cross was broken,
The crown of pain to three and thirty years …
But this I know, all flesh shall see his glory,
And he shall reap the harvest he has sown,
And some glad day his sun shall shine in splendour
When he the Saviour, Saviour of the world is known.

I cannot tell how all the lands shall worship …
But this I know, the skies will thrill with rapture,
And myriad, myriad human voices sing,
And earth to heaven, and heaven to earth,
will answer:
At last the Saviour, Saviour of the world is King!

William Young Fullerton (1857-1932)

SATURDAY

Isaiah 50 v 4-9

Have you ever been accused of meddling when you were only trying to help? It can be a painful experience. Or have you ever received a hostile reaction for telling someone about Christ's love? Goodness and truth are not always well received.

In this third song it's becoming clear that the servant will *suffer*. He will be beaten, struck, mocked and spat on (v 6). It's not hard to hear in this description the echo of its fulfilment in the last hours of Jesus' life. What this song makes clear is:

1. Suffering is part of the Father's plan. "I have not been rebellious," says Jesus the Servant (v 5). It's a statement sandwiched between the instruction of the Lord in verse 4 and the hostility of humanity in verse 6. The point is clear: Jesus faced suffering in obedience to his Father's plan.

2. Suffering can be faced with God's help. Suffering is the servant's choice. "I offered my back to those who beat me ... I did not hide my face from mocking and spitting" (v 6). Jesus was not dragged kicking and screaming to the cross. "I set my face like flint," he says in verse 7. It's a powerful statement of his resolution.

This resolution is made with the help of God. That's the logic of verse 7:

> *Because the Sovereign LORD helps me,*
> *I will not be disgraced.*
> *Therefore have I set my face like flint,*
> *and I know I will not be put to shame.*

The shame and disgrace here are not that of the cross itself. Quite the opposite. It would have been shameful if Jesus had turned away from the cross, disobeyed God and not followed through the plan of salvation. But he didn't turn away. Jesus could face the cross with resolution because the Holy Spirit strengthened him. Christ, says Hebrews 9 v 14, "through the eternal Spirit offered himself unblemished to God".

3. Suffering is not the final verdict. Jesus didn't avoid suffering because he looked beyond the suffering to his vindication. "He who vindicates me is near," he says (Isaiah 50 v 8). On earth Jesus and his accusers faced off (v 8). And it looked as if his accusers had won. But the verdict of heaven is completely different and it's heaven's verdict which will prevail. Ultimately it's his accusers who will "wear out like a garment" (v 9).

This is the most intimate of the servant songs. But we don't need to feel embarrassed about listening in. Verse 4 suggests Jesus the Servant wants his example to help others, and in verses 10-11 God exhorts us to follow the Servant's lead. This is intended to be a "word that sustains the weary" (v 4). We don't suffer to redeem the world in the way Jesus did. But we are called to deny ourselves, take up our cross and follow Christ.

So let's retrace our steps. What's "the word that sustains" here for us?

1. Suffering is part of the Father's plan. Our suffering doesn't mean our lives are out of control. God is using our suffering to advance his kingdom and refine our hearts.

2. Suffering can be faced with God's help. We are not left to face suffering alone. The Spirit empowers us to endure.

3. Suffering is not the final verdict. "I consider that our present sufferings are not worth comparing with the glory that will be revealed in us" (Romans 8 v 18).

Meditate

Therefore we do not lose heart.
Though outwardly we are wasting away,
yet inwardly we are being renewed day by day.
For our light and momentary troubles
are achieving for us an eternal glory
that far outweighs them all.
So we fix our eyes not on what is seen,
but on what is unseen,
since what is seen is temporary,
but what is unseen is eternal.

2 Corinthians 4 v 16-18

We've looked briefly at the first three of Isaiah's four servant songs. For the next six weeks we will slow down to look in depth at his final and greatest servant song…

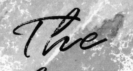

THE FIRST WEEK OF LENT

The Exaltation

SUNDAY

Isaiah 52 v 13-15

Isaiah makes some amazing promises in chapters 51 and 52. God is going to comfort his people and liberate them from their captivity. He's going to bring them home and make their home like a new Garden of Eden (51 v 3). His salvation will last for ever, longer than the earth itself (51 v 6). God will remove from his people the cup of his wrath (51 v 22). In other words, God will solve the problem of their sin.

All of which raises the question: *How?* How can any of this be achieved? Or perhaps the question is: *Who?* Who can bring this about? And God's answer is, "See, my servant" (52 v 13). It's an invitation to look at Jesus.

But all is not what it seems. Appearances are going to be deceptive.

Pray

Pray through the reading by taking a phrase or two at a time. Each time identify…
* *something to praise God for*
* *something to confess*
* *something to turn into a request*

MONDAY

*Just as there were many who were appalled at him—his
appearance was so disfigured beyond that of any human
being and his form marred beyond human likeness...
(Isaiah 52 v 14)*

M y wife loves listening to *The Archers*, the world's
longest running radio soap opera. Once styled
as "an everyday story of country folk", its tagline is
now "contemporary drama in a rural setting".

Before each episode, the radio announcer introduces
it with a short summary of what's going on. "David and
Ruth are discussing the latest milk yields while Linda is
trying to drum up support for the village play." You get
the idea. It's just enough to orient you to what's coming.
It is, after all, a radio drama so there are no visual clues.
We have to be told what's happening. We can't recognise
the characters from their appearance.

That's what God is doing in these verses. We need
some help to get our bearings. We have to be told what's
happening.

But we need this cue not just because we're only hearing
words. We need this cue because straight away we discover
the servant's "appearance was ... disfigured beyond that
of any human being and his form marred beyond human

likeness" (v 14). Even if this were a television drama and we could see the central character, we wouldn't recognise him. Right from the start, we're given a clue that all is not what it seems. When we look at the cross of Jesus, appearances are going to be deceptive.

Think of Jesus hanging on the cross. On the night before, he had been flogged, the whip tearing into his skin. A crown of thorns had been shoved onto his brow so that blood ran down his face. In the morning, the beam of the cross was strapped to his shoulders and he had staggered through the streets until he had collapsed in exhaustion. At the point of execution, the nails were driven into wrists and feet, and he was hoisted up until the cross dropped with a jarring jolt into its slot. Hanging from his arms, it was impossible to breathe without pushing up on the nails in his feet to release the pressure on his lungs. By this point "his appearance was so disfigured beyond that of any human being and his form marred beyond human likeness" (v 14).

Yet the first thing we learn about the servant is that he's wise. "See, my servant will act wisely" (v 13). He knows what he's doing. If this is wisdom, then it's not like any wisdom we've ever seen before. This wisdom is appalling—quite literally.

When we are first introduced to the servant in Isaiah 42 v 1, he is announced with a declaration of God's delight in him: "Here is my servant, whom I uphold, my chosen one in whom I delight". But now he is greeted with human revulsion. "There were many who were appalled at him," says 52 v 14.

The word "appalled" is used elsewhere of a devastated city (Ezekiel 27 v 35). Think of news footage of disasters: the rubble of bombed-out buildings; the mangled wreckage of earthquakes; the debris left by hurricanes. They have a strange fascination. We can't look—and we can't look away. They both appal and appeal. God had devastated the city. And now God is devastating his own servant.

What kind of wisdom is this? As you prepare to explore this servant song, ask God to help you find out.

Meditate

Christ's deformity is what gives form to you.
If he had been unwilling to be deformed,
you would never have got back the form you lost.
So he hung on the cross, deformed,
but his deformity was our beauty.

Augustine (354-430)

TUESDAY

See, my servant will act wisely.
(Isaiah 52 v 13)

We stand before the cross in confusion. What's this all about? How can this be an act of God? We come with our assumptions about who God is, and then we look at the cross and conclude: this can't be God. How can this be divine wisdom and power?

Paul provides his own commentary on the strange wisdom of the cross in 1 Corinthians 1 v 18-25:

> *For the message of the cross is foolishness to those who are perishing, but to us who are being saved it is the power of God. For it is written:*
>
> > *"I will destroy the wisdom of the wise;*
> > *the intelligence of the intelligent I will frustrate."*
>
> *Where is the wise person? Where is the teacher of the law? Where is the philosopher of this age? Has not God made foolish the wisdom of the world? For since in the wisdom of God the world through its wisdom did not know him, God was pleased through the foolishness of what was preached to save those who believe. Jews demand signs and Greeks look for wisdom, but we preach Christ crucified: a stumbling-block to Jews and foolishness to Gentiles, but to those whom God has called, both Jews and Greeks, Christ the power of God and the wisdom of God. For the foolishness of God is wiser than human wisdom, and the weakness of God is stronger than human strength.*

This passage was central to the thoughts of the great Reformer Martin Luther. Luther recognised that the righteousness of God turns our notions of "rightness" upside down. We think righteousness or justice means giving people what they deserve. And, indeed, that is how God will exercise righteousness on the day of judgment. But the righteousness of God revealed in the gospel is a gift from God through which he counts us righteous in Christ. Because we're *in Christ*, we have the same status as Christ. Christ is perfectly righteous and therefore so are we. Christ is vindicated by God and therefore so are we. Christ is right with God and therefore so are we.

But that means something utterly unexpected happens: God treats unrighteous people as though they're righteous. The cross has turned our perceptions and conceptions upside down.

What Luther recognised is that this is not only true of human notions of justice, but also of human notions of power, triumph, glory and wisdom. All our proud notions are undermined when we stand before the cross. We think we're clever enough to know God. We think we're good enough to be right with God. We think we're strong enough to please God. But the cross sends these notions tumbling across the floor like a spilt bowl of fruit.

The cross shows we've misunderstood God. We assume a god—if there is such a thing—will be a being of power and splendour. What we see in the cross is weakness, defeat and shame. And our instinct is to turn away. But resist that urge for a moment and take a good look. What we see is a God more loving than we could have ever imagined:

- *A God who is willing to exchange the glory of heaven for the shame of the cross;*

- *A God who is willing to exchange the safety of heaven for the pain of the cross;*
- *A God who is willing to exchange the power of heaven for the weakness of the cross.*

To any self-interested person this looks like utter folly. But God is not self-interested. He is self-giving love. And to self-giving love, this is wisdom. For through the cross, God rescues the people he loves.

The Lord Jesus endured the shame, pain and weakness of the cross for you. How will you remember this today?

Meditate

O sacred Head, now wounded,
With grief and shame weighed down;
Now scornfully surrounded
With thorns, thine only crown.
O sacred Head, what glory,
What bliss till now was thine!
Yet, though despised and gory, I joy to call thee mine.

What thou, my Lord, hast suffered,
Was all for sinners' gain.
Mine, mine was the transgression,
But thine the deadly pain.
Lo, here I fall, my Saviour! 'Tis I deserve thy place;
Look on me with thy favour, Vouchsafe to me thy grace.

Paulus Gerhardt (1607-1676),
translated by James W. Alexander (1804-1859)

WEDNESDAY

And kings will shut their mouths because of him.
(Isaiah 52 v 15)

I wonder if you've ever stood in a hall of mirrors. Curved mirrors reflect strange inverted reflections back at you. You appear fattened into a ball; then stretched up into a pole; then flipped upside-down.

The cross is like a strange reverse mirror. "Mirror, mirror on the wall," we cry, "who is the greatest of them all?" And the cross gives a topsy-turvy answer. If you think you're strong, then you see weakness reflected back to you. If you think you're wise, then you see folly. But if you recognise your weakness and confusion, then you see Christ, the power of God and the wisdom of God (1 Corinthians 1 v 24).

Yesterday we saw how the cross shows we've misunderstood God. Now we discover *the cross shows we've misunderstood ourselves*. All our proud notions of power, triumph, glory and wisdom are turned on their heads. All the things for which we so routinely strive evaporate at the foot of the cross. We think we're clever enough to know God. We think we're good enough to be right with God. We think we're strong enough to please God. But God would not have let his Son die if we could have saved ourselves. God would not have given up his beloved Son in an empty gesture. Jesus died for us because there is no other way. We are not, and can never be, wise enough to know God or good enough to be right with God or strong enough to please God. So it is that the cross humbles us.

Many people, says Paul, demand signs and look for wisdom (1 Corinthians 1 v 22). They think God will be found in a display of power or the intricacies of phi-losophy: "If we could do more miracles, then people would turn to Christ". Or the secret to making Christ known, we imagine, is matching human philosophy intellectual blow for intellectual blow.

What Paul realised is that God hides his glory in the shame of the cross. Why? So no one can claim to know God because they're clever, or claim to be right with God because they're good, or claim to please God because they're capable. The clever and the good and the capable (or at least those who suppose themselves to be so) just don't get it. It's only through *faith* that people see the glory of the cross. And therefore it's only by God's grace. "Therefore, as it is written: 'Let the one who boasts boast in the Lord' " (1 Corinthians 1 v 31).

If you find the cross confusing, or you find it odd that Christians boast in a horrendous death, then it may be because you have:

- *a wrong view of yourself—you're far more needy than you ever realised; or...*
- *a wrong view of God—he is far more loving than you ever realised.*

Paul quotes God's words from another portion of Isaiah: "I will destroy the wisdom of the wise; the intelligence of the intelligent I will frustrate" (1 Corinthians 1 v 19; Isaiah 29 v 14).

The cross is where human wisdom unravels. This is what Isaiah means when he says, "Kings will shut their mouths because of him" (52 v 15). In the end the cross will silence all our human pretensions. We think we are clever enough, good enough or strong enough for God. Meanwhile, in stark contrast, Jesus, the Servant of the Lord, hangs on the cross. And Paul, his great apostle, disavowed "eloquence or human wisdom". Instead Paul resolved "to know nothing while I was with you except Jesus Christ and him crucified" (1 Corinthians 2 v 1-2).

What about *you*? What are you resolved to know? What's your boast?

Meditate

Mirrors that hide nothing hurt me.
They reveal an ugliness I'd rather deny ...

My wife is such a mirror.
When I have sinned against her,
my sin appears in the suffering of her face.
Her tears reflect with terrible accuracy
my selfishness. My self! ...

"Stop crying!" I command,
as though the mirror were at fault.
Or else I just leave the room. Walk away.
O, what a coward I am, and what a fool!
Only when I have the courage fully to look,
clearly to know myself—even the evil of myself—
will I admit my need for healing …

The passion of Christ, his suffering and his death,
is such a mirror.
Are the tears of my dear wife hard to look at?
Well, the pain in the face of Jesus is harder.
It is my self in my extremist truth. My sinful self …

So that's what I see reflected
in the mirror of Christ's crucifixion: my death.
My rightful punishment.
My sin and its just consequence.
Me.

Walter Wangerin (b. 1944)

THURSDAY

He will be raised and lifted up and highly exalted.
(Isaiah 52 v 13)

This verse looks more promising. We're all aware of how kings and queens are raised up. The British monarch is crowned on a raised platform to ensure that, even when the monarch is seated, he or she is above everyone else. So they "ascend" to the throne—quite literally. Members of the royal family are known as "Your Royal Highness" because their social status is meant to be higher than the rest of us.

And here is God's servant being raised, lifted and exalted—one, two, three times higher than the rest of us. What could be more regal? Here is his glory for all to see.

But again, all is not what it seems. At one point during his time on earth, Jesus said, "And I, when I am lifted up from the earth, will draw all people to myself" (John 12 v 32). It's a clear echo of this servant song and indeed, a few verses later, John quotes from the song itself (v 38). Here is Jesus about to ascend to his throne.

Except that John adds a little editorial comment: "He said this to show the kind of death he was going to die" (v 33). John is playing on the fact that people were lifted up when hung on a Roman cross. From a Roman point of view, the executed criminal was raised above the crowd so everyone could see justice being done. Each crucifixion was a deterrent that all could see. But for John, the cross is the *glory* of Jesus. Jesus is raised, lifted and exalted *on the cross*.

This really is upside down or perhaps it is downside up. In an amazing act of love, Jesus sacrificed himself to win his people. And *this* is his glory. Jesus is glorified for and through his self-giving love. This is a glory that turns our notions of God upside down. It's a glory that cannot be matched.

John has in mind what Jesus said to Nicodemus, a Jewish leader who visited him at night. Jesus said, "Just as Moses lifted up the snake in the wilderness, so the Son of Man must be lifted up, that everyone who believes may have eternal life in him" (John 3 v 14-15). Many centuries before, when the people of Israel "spoke against God", God had sent venomous snakes among them in judgment. But God had also told Moses to lift up a bronze snake on a pole. Everyone who looked to the snake was saved (Numbers 21 v 4-9).

It was a picture of Jesus. Everyone who looks to Jesus, lifted up on the cross, will be saved from God's judgment. Jesus is not honoured *despite* his humiliation, but *because* of his humiliation. The shame of the cross is the glory of Jesus because through it Jesus gives eternal life to all who believe in him. In this way, Jesus will draw all the people of the world to himself.

Meditate

The Son of God was made the Son of man
that the sons of men might become the sons of God.
He took our misery that
we might have his glory.
He was born of a woman,
that we might be born of God.
Christ was really sin for us
that we might be really righteous in him.

Thomas Manton (1620-1677)

FRIDAY

So he will sprinkle many nations.
(Isaiah 52 v 15)

I love having a bath. A shower is great if you're in a hurry. But you need a bath to feel really clean. And warm. And relaxed.

But what about deep-down clean? What can cleanse our hearts?

Sprinkling was a temple activity which signified cleansing and consecration:

- *"Take the Levites from among all the Israelites and make them ceremonially clean. To purify them, do this: sprinkle the water of cleansing on them" (Numbers 8 v 6-7).*

- *"Then Moses took the anointing oil and anointed the tabernacle and everything in it, and so consecrated them" (Leviticus 8 v 10).*
- *"Seven times [the priest] shall sprinkle the one to be cleansed of the defiling disease, and then pronounce them clean" (Leviticus 14 v 7).*

But Jesus is not sprinkling Levites or the tabernacle or even the people of Israel. He is sprinkling many nations (Isaiah 52 v 15).

Isaiah is echoing an outrageous idea he had proclaimed back in 19 v 19-25. There he had talked about how God would "strike Egypt with a plague". Nothing too surprising about that. After all, that had happened before during the exodus—ten times before, in fact (Exodus 7 – 12). At this point every Israelite is cheering—the great enemy is going to get it in the neck. But then Isaiah adds, "He will strike them and heal them. They will turn to the LORD, and he will respond to their pleas and heal them" (19 v 22).

In verse 20 Isaiah says, "When they cry out to the LORD because of their oppressors, he will send them a saviour and defender, and he will rescue them." Again, this is exodus language. That's exactly what happened at the exodus. Indeed, that's pretty much how the book of Exodus described it (Exodus 2 v 23-24; 3 v 7-9). Except Isaiah is not talking about Israel; he's talking about Egypt. It's the Egyptians who will cry out to the LORD, and it's to the Egyptians that God will send a saviour.

Who are the LORD's people? Isaiah's contemporaries knew the answer: Israel, the children of Abraham, the tribes of Jacob. But Isaiah says a day is coming when the LORD will call Egypt "my people". It's so audacious. Did Isaiah drop his voice as he said these words? Did his face turn red? Did he fear arrest for troublemaking?

All this is echoed in this promise to sprinkle many nations. In the sacrificial system, the external body was a symbol of the soul. For example, leprosy and menstruation made you unclean—not because leprosy or menstruation are sinful, but because they were symbols of the state of the human soul. Our sin taints us. So human beings need to be made pure if we're to approach God.

One feature of this symbolism was the prohibition of disfigured Levites serving as priests. A priest had to have a flawless body. But the servant in Isaiah 52 is disfigured (v 14). He ought to be considered impure. And in one sense he is. He is disfigured because he's taking our impurities on himself. And so, through his disfigurement, he makes us clean. His death leads to the sprinkling of many nations—to their cleanliness and consecration.

In verse 14 "many" are appalled at the disfigured servant. In verse 15 "many" nations are cleaned through his blood. The repeat of the word "many" captures the contrast between appearance and reality. Many find his appearance appalling; but there are also many who find him beautiful. Many see a man dying in defeat; but there are also many who see the victory of God's people. Many see a man disfigured beyond recognition; but there are also many who look to him and are made whole.

Who do *you* see, and what would you like to say to him right now?

Meditate

Thy works, not mine, O Christ,
Speak gladness to this heart;
They tell me all is done,
They bid my fear depart.

Thy pains, not mine, O Christ,
Upon the shameful tree,
Have paid the law's full price
And purchased peace for me.

Thy cross, not mine, O Christ,
Has borne the awful load
Of sins that none in heav'n
Or earth could bear but God.

Thy death, not mine, O Christ,
Has paid the ransom due;
Ten thousand deaths like mine
Would have been all too few.

Thy righteousness, O Christ,
Alone can cover me:
No righteousness avails
Save that which is of thee.

To whom, save thee, who canst alone
For sin atone, Lord, shall I flee?

Horatius Bonar (1808-1889)

SATURDAY

*For what they were not told, they will see,
and what they have not heard, they will understand.
(Isaiah 52 v 15)*

We began this servant song with an invitation to "see": *See, my servant* (52 v 13). What do you see when you look at Jesus? What do you see when you look at the cross? How do you navigate your way through this strange wisdom that defies appearances?

Seeing and not seeing has been a big theme throughout Isaiah's ministry. It all starts with his call in Isaiah 6. Here's the message Isaiah is told to proclaim: "Be ever hearing, but never understanding; be ever seeing, but never perceiving" (6 v 9). It's not much of a commission! Isaiah's job is not to win converts. Quite the opposite. His job is to confirm people in their rebellion (6 v 10). People who refuse to listen to God will become deaf. People who refuse to see his servant will become blind. You may have seen this in action as you have witnessed people becoming hardened in their rejection of God and increasingly hostile to his people.

God is hiding himself from the self-reliant and self-willed. It turns out he's hiding himself in plain sight—on the cross. There God's glory and power and wisdom are on display for all to see. But human pride sees only shame and weakness and folly.

What hope is there when the more people hear, the less they listen? The answer comes in the form of a surprising reversal. "For what they were not told, they will see, and what they have not heard, they will understand." (52 v 15)

The problem is people who hear but don't understand, who see but don't perceive (6 v 9). But now the promise is that people who *don't* hear will understand, and people who *haven't* been told will see. People who were never looking for God will find God—or rather, be found by God.

This is our story. None of us set out on a grand quest for God. But God sent a Christian friend into your life, or a moment of crisis that pushed you beyond yourself, or a Christian parent who pointed you to Jesus. Even if you were searching for God, it was because he had first implanted that longing in your heart. Or maybe you haven't found God. Yet here you are reading these words and hearing God's invitation.

It's sometimes said that attending church can give you just enough religion to inoculate you against the message of Jesus. In other words, churches are full of people who think their morality or rituals make them right with God. Or they've domesticated and tamed God so that he offers no threat. They've rubbed out the need for the cross. If it stands for anything, it's a sign of divine love or a model of self-giving. The cross no longer saves them because they no longer think they need saving. Meanwhile, the saving message of the cross goes to those who previously were not looking for God.

This has been fulfilled many times over in history. The Jews as a nation rejected Jesus as their Messiah, so the gospel went to Gentiles. As the West, once powerfully influenced by Christianity, becomes increasingly secular, the church is growing across the southern hemisphere. "God chose the foolish things of the world to shame the wise; God chose the weak things of the world to shame the strong" (1 Corinthians 1 v 27).

Paul quoted these words from Isaiah 52 as he appealed to the church in Rome for help in his mission to Spain (Romans 15 v 20-21). These words are a mandate for global mission and a promise that it will succeed. Many who are currently unreached by the gospel will see in Jesus the servant of God and "he will sprinkle many nations" (Isaiah 52 v 15). Why not pray for one of those nations now?

Meditate

Look, ye saints! The sight is glorious:
See the Man of Sorrows now;
From the fight returned victorious,
Every knee to him shall bow;
Crown him, crown him,
Crowns become the Victor's brow.

Sinners in derision scorned him,
Mocking thus the Saviour's claim;
Saints and angels crowd around him,
Own his title, praise his name;
Crown him, crown him,
Spread abroad the Victor's fame.

Thomas Kelly (1769-1855)

THE SECOND WEEK OF LENT

The Sorrow

SUNDAY
Isaiah 53 v 1-3

Suffering can be a lonely experience. It's bad enough facing illness, unemployment, bereavement or divorce. But it's often made harder because people don't really know what to do with you. They don't know what to say. They try to sympathise, but they struggle—unless they've been through something similar. It's easier for them to find someone else to talk to. They don't want to be confronted with your misery.

Where can we turn? To whom can we go?

"See, my servant," says God at the beginning of this song. And what we see when we look at Jesus is "a man of suffering" (v 3). We discover someone who is "familiar with pain". Someone like us. Someone who can sympathise. Someone you can talk to, right now.

Pray
Pray through the reading by taking a phrase or two at a time. Each time identify…
- *something to praise God for*
- *something to confess*
- *something to turn into a request*

MONDAY

He grew up before him like a tender shoot,
and like a root out of dry ground.
(Isaiah 53 v 2)

I love chopping wood. Catch it just right and the axe slices through the log. It's very pleasing. "Grab the next piece," shouts my axe. It's in charge. I'm just the instrument it uses to bring itself down on the wood.

That, of course, is ridiculous. The tool is not the master. Yet it's a mistake we make more often than we realise.

In 722 BC the Assyrian Empire swept through the Middle East. In the process they defeated and destroyed the northern tribes of Israel. Not only had Isaiah predicted this, but God describes Assyria as "the rod of my anger" (10 v 5). God was using Assyria to judge his people.

But Isaiah had also warned Assyria not to get above themselves. It was, after all, only the tool—not the master wielding it (10 v 15). But Assyria paid no attention to the God of Israel. So this is what Isaiah said:

> *See, the Lord, the LORD Almighty,*
> *will lop off the boughs with great power.*
> *The lofty trees will be felled,*
> *the tall ones will be brought low.*

> *He will cut down the forest thickets with an axe;*
> *Lebanon will fall before the Mighty One.*
> *(Isaiah 10 v 33-34)*

The axe that Assyria wielded to bring down Israel would be turned on Assyria. In their pride they would be brought low.

We, too, are tools in the hands of God. It's a great privilege. But we must never forget who is the tool and who is the Master. Is that something you need to repent of?

The result of God's judgment against both Israel and Assyria is a barren wasteland. If you've ever seen a forest cleared, you'll be able to visualise the scene. In dense woodland the canopy of leaves prevents light reaching ground level, so little grows. Remove the trees, and all that remain are tree stumps in barren soil. This is the scene after God has passed through in judgment.

But in the midst of the wilderness, Isaiah continues with this promise: "A shoot will come up from the stump of Jesse; from his roots a Branch will bear fruit" (11 v 1). Jesse was the father of King David, Israel's greatest king. From the remnants of David's family a new king will come up, like a shoot in the wilderness. The Spirit of the Lord will be upon this king, says Isaiah, so that he will reign in justice and peace (11 v 2-11). The enemies of God's people will be brought low like felled trees. And the king of God's people will have been raised high.

It's this glorious vision of a future king that Isaiah evokes in 53 v 2: "He grew up before him like a tender shoot, and like a root out of dry ground." But the shoot of 11 v 1 has become a "tender shoot" in 53 v 2. This king looks so fragile. He doesn't appear like a majestic cedar or a sturdy oak. One misplaced footstep and it might all be over; one hungry bovine and this shoot will be gone. Moreover, all around him is devastation—the dry ground left by God's judgment. How can a kingdom be rebuilt from these ruins? How can glory return to this devastated place?

So it is that Jesus is born in a borrowed manger. There is no pomp, at least not on earth. The choirs of heaven fanfare his birth, but on earth his only court is a group of shepherds. Then, almost immediately, he's on the run—a refugee from state oppression. Meanwhile God's people are under the thumb of the Roman Empire. God's people are still sinful and God's judgment has not gone away. All our hopes rest on this child. Yet he looks so fragile in the barren wasteland of our sin.

Meditate

For he whom you now treat with contempt
was once above you.
He who is now made man was once the Unmade.
What he was he continued to be;
what he was not he took to himself.
In the beginning he was uncaused;
for what is the cause of God?
But afterwards for a cause he was born.
And that cause was that you might be saved.

Gregory of Nazianzus

TUESDAY

He had no beauty or majesty to attract us to him,
nothing in his appearance that we should desire him.
(Isaiah 53 v 2)

If you saw Jesus on the first Christmas Day, what would you have concluded? Another baby. Likely to become a carpenter like his dad. A poor, northern tradesman. Nothing special. The shepherds and foreign visitors might have made you wonder if you'd hung round to listen to their tales of angels and stars. But you'd seen nothing to confirm their claims. All you'd seen is a baby. It would never occur to you that you'd just seen a king.

Isaiah says, "He grew up before him like a tender shoot" (v 2). Before whom? It must be the LORD, whose arm has been revealed in the previous verse. To humanity, poking its head round the stable door, Jesus looked nothing special. But before God he is the beginning of a new kingdom, a new era, a new hope. God pokes his head round the stable door, as it were, and sees his eternal Son, the Word made flesh, the coming Saviour-King, born to redeem his people and restore God's reign.

Over a thousand years before Isaiah, Abraham's grandson Jacob had a dream in which he saw a stairway to heaven with angels "ascending and descending" (Genesis

28 v 12). "Ascending" is the same word that is translated as "grew up" in Isaiah 53 v 2. The origins of Jesus were so fragile, so humble, so ordinary. But the trajectory was upwards. Jesus would one day ascend to receive all authority and all honour. "In that day the Branch of the LORD will be beautiful and glorious, and the fruit of the land will be the pride and glory of the survivors in Israel" (4 v 2).

That is what God sees in the baby in the manger. But not us. Not yet. For Isaiah continues, "He had no beauty or majesty to attract us to him, nothing in his appearance that we should desire him" (53 v 2).

Isaiah isn't claiming that the servant would be especially ugly. Indeed, he isn't really saying anything about the appearance of Jesus. That's the point. There's nothing to say. There was nothing in the physical appearance of Jesus to make him stand out. He wasn't taller than others. He wasn't better looking. He wasn't imposing. His words and his actions would have made him stand out, for sure, but not his appearance. If you'd walked past him in the street, you wouldn't have picked him out from the crowd.

Jesus looked just like anyone else because he *was* just like anyone else. He wasn't some super-human, an advanced version of the species, some unique evolutionary adaptation. He worked for his living—just as we do. He was hungry—just as we are. He was misunderstood—just as we are. He grew tired—just as we do. He laughed at jokes—just as we do. He fell ill—just as we do. He could be disappointed—just as we are. He was betrayed by friends—just as we are.

He was just as we are. The only difference is that he didn't sin. "We have one who has been tempted in every way, just as we are—yet he did not sin" (Hebrews 4 v 15). He was one of us. And he's one of us still. His resurrection and ascension have not reduced his humanity.

Meditate

Sinner, you have not to come to an absolute God;
you are not invited to draw near to the consuming fire.
You might well tremble to approach
him whom you have so grievously offended.
But there is a man ordained to mediate
between you and God,
and if you would come to God,
you must come through him—the man Christ Jesus ...

He is a man with hands full of blessing,
eyes wet with tears of pity,
lips overflowing with love,
and a heart melting with tenderness.
Do you not see the gash in his side?
Through that wound there is a highway to his heart.
O sinners, the way to the Saviour's heart is open,
and penitent seekers shall never be denied!
Why should the most despairing
be afraid to approach the Saviour?
He has deigned to assume the character
of the Lamb of God—
and I have never known even a little child
who was afraid of a lamb.

C. H. Spurgeon (1834-1892)

WEDNESDAY

He was despised and rejected by mankind,
a man of suffering, and familiar with pain.
(Isaiah 53 v 3)

A young woman poked her head in. "Can I come
in?" She smiled, all bright and breezy. She was a
counsellor, she explained, and had come to talk to us
about therapeutic support available to families in our
situation. Rebecca took against her on sight.

In *Thinking Out Loud*, the England soccer player Rio
Ferdinand describes the loss of his wife, Rebecca, to
cancer. Rebecca grew close to the nursing staff who
cared for her. The one exception was the counsellor.

"Tell me this," Rebecca asked her coldly. "Have you
ever lost someone close to you?" "Well, no, I can't say I
have," the young woman replied. "But I have trained."
Without another word, Rebecca shifted onto her side
to face the wall, and after a few awkward minutes the
counsellor backed sheepishly out of the room. "Don't
let her anywhere near my kids," Rebecca told me flatly,
once she had gone. "What the hell does she know? She's
never had to live through anything like this. What a
pointless waste of time."

Not only was Jesus fully human; he was also a *suffering* human being. He was, as the King James Version famously puts it, a "man of sorrows". He shared our humanity and he shared our pain. It was familiar to him. "My soul is overwhelmed with sorrow to the point of death," he said on the night before he died (Matthew 26 v 38). "Grief was his intimate, inseparable companion," says John Newton.

This is Christ's love for us. All this he willingly accepted because his love made him determined to save us. And this is the beginning of our love for him. We love because he first loved us. Meditate on the Saviour's love for you, see his sufferings as the measure of that love, and your love for him will grow.

Remember Rebecca Ferdinand's words: "What the hell does she know? She's never had to live through anything like this. What a pointless waste of time." The counsellor had been "trained". But it's only by experiencing suffering ourselves that we are truly equipped to empathise with others. And Jesus has been equipped through suffering to sympathise with you in your suffering. "It was fitting that God," says Hebrews 2 v 10, "should make the pioneer of their salvation perfect through what he suffered". Jesus does know; he has lived through suffering; he is never a pointless waste of time.

It also means *our* suffering need not be a pointless waste of time. It may be that God is equipping us to "comfort those in any trouble with the comfort we ourselves receive from God" (2 Corinthians 1 v 4). Don't use your suffering to exclude the world. Use it to connect to others so you can receive comfort from God *through* others and offer comfort from God *to* others.

Meditate

One there is, above all others,
Well deserves the name of Friend;
His is love beyond a brother's,
Costly, free, and knows no end:
They who once his kindness prove,
Find it everlasting love!

Which of all our friends to save us,
Could or would have shed their blood?
But our Jesus died to have us
Reconciled in him to God:
This was boundless love indeed!
Jesus is a Friend in need.

O for grace our hearts to soften!
Teach us, Lord, at length to love.
We, alas, forget too often,
What a Friend we have above.
But when home our souls are brought,
We will love thee as we ought.

John Newton (1725-1807)

THURSDAY

He was despised and rejected by mankind,
a man of suffering, and familiar with pain.
Like one from whom people hide their faces
he was despised, and we held him in low esteem.
(Isaiah 53 v 3)

Jesus is God with us, God suffering with us, true God made true man. But this is not Isaiah's main point in these verses. Isaiah is explaining why so few people have believed his message (v 1). Why have they not been drawn to this wonderful King? Perhaps that's a question you ask too.

Verses 1-3 tell the story of Jesus. He was born a king, but there were few signs of his royal status. For 30 years he was an ordinary human being—not someone who would stand out from the crowd. Then he began his ministry, and for three years he was despised and rejected. His ministry brought him to humanity's attention and we didn't like what we saw. In verses 4-6 this hostility would reach its climax at the cross.

Jesus came to be one with us and we despised him for it. "He came to that which was his own," says John 1 v 11, "but his own did not receive him". When true love appeared among us, we hated it. When true beauty appeared, we found nothing in it to attract us. God in

Christ came to stand *with* us—in our pain, in our plight, in our sin. And in response, we stood *against* God. God with us; us against God. Jesus came to be on our side, and we started playing against him, fouling our own player and kicking the ball in the wrong direction.

Think about how people responded to Jesus during his life on earth. Right from the start, there was no room for Jesus in our world. He had to be born and laid in a manger (Luke 2 v 7). It wasn't long before the authorities were trying to murder Jesus, and he had to become a refugee (Matthew 2 v 13-16). When he was an adult, his own family thought he was insane, while the religious leaders accused him of being satanic (Mark 3 v 21-22). Jesus had nowhere to lay his head and nowhere to call home (Luke 9 v 58).

As his life came to an end, he was betrayed by a friend and abandoned by his followers (Matthew 26 v 47-56). The Jewish council condemned him as a blasphemer; the crowds bayed for his death; and the Roman governor sentenced him to a terrorist's execution (Matthew 26 v 65-66; Luke 23 v 22-25). The soldiers mocked Jesus with an ironic scarlet robe and crown of thorns, spitting on his face and striking his head (Matthew 27 v 27-31). And then at the end, they drove nails through his flesh and hoisted him as an object of scorn (Luke 23 v 33-37). Such was the malice and spite directed towards one whose every act was an act of love. Truly Jesus was "despised and rejected by mankind".

These are not the actions of someone else or a rogue few. Isaiah won't let us off the hook so easily. He uses first-person pronouns—"we" and "us". Every one of us is implicated. "He was despised and rejected by *mankind*" (v 3). We're all culpable. We may not have been in the crowd that cried, "Crucify him". But we've all pushed Christ out of our lives.

Think of the times when you've neglected his words or despised his people or disobeyed his will or denied his name. Really—stop now and think…

Jesus has been presented to you, and you've turned away in boredom or anger or scorn or fear.

Still, today, people despise the message of Jesus for being vulgar, simple and plain. We want a Christianity that's sophisticated, highbrow and cultured, so that we can feel good about how sophisticated, highbrow and cultured we are.

Here's the great irony: *we've turned the very fact that Jesus identifies with us into a reason to reject him.* He has become an ordinary human being, and we claim he's too ordinary. "Isn't this the carpenter's son?" we say (Matthew 13 v 55). "Who do you think you are?" we ask (John 8 v 53). Too ordinary.

"Have any of the rulers or the Pharisees believed in him?" the Pharisees ask at one point (John 7 v 48). No one with influence or education backs him. Too ordinary.

He came as one of us and we despised him for it.

Meditate

The cross of Christ displays
the divine perfections with peculiar glory.

Here the name of God is revealed,
as a just God and a Saviour.
Here the believer contemplates, in one view,
the unspeakable evil of sin,
and the unsearchable riches of mercy.

This gives us the most affecting sense
of the misery which we deserve,
while at the same time we receive the fullest assurance
that there is forgiveness with God.

We discover a sure foundation
upon which we may build our hope of eternal life,
without fear of disappointment.

John Newton (1725-1807)

FRIDAY

*Who has believed our message and to whom
has the arm of the* LORD *been revealed?
(Isaiah 53 v 1)*

I t's not the first time Isaiah has reflected on how his message has been received. In 28 v 9-10 he records what the people are saying about his ministry:

> *⁹ "Who is it he is trying to teach? To whom is he explaining his message? To children weaned from their milk, to those just taken from the breast?*
> *¹⁰ For it is: do this, do that, a rule for this, a rule for that; a little here, a little there."*

This is a message for children and idiots, they say. Verse 10 is impossible to translate—it's a babble of nonsense as the people mock the nonsense they claim is coming out of Isaiah's mouth. Today we might say, "Blah, blah, blah—on and on he goes without ever making sense".

In response God says that, since his people treat his word as nonsense, then nonsense is what they'll hear (28 v 11-13). Instead of his gentle invitation to find rest in him, they'll hear the "blah, blah, blah" of a foreign army. The chatter on the streets of Israel will all be in Assyrian as they are overrun by the Assyrian army. Let's see what sense they make of that!

Instead of looking to God for help, the people of Judah are scurrying off to do a deal with Egypt. Again Isaiah quotes what they're saying: "You boast, 'We have entered into a covenant with death, with the realm of the dead we have made an agreement. When an overwhelming scourge sweeps by, it cannot touch us, for we have made a lie our refuge and falsehood our hiding-place'" (28 v 15). I doubt very much that these were words the people actually used. I suspect they said, *We have entered into a covenant with Pharaoh ... we have made Egypt our refuge*. But Isaiah names this for what it is: a covenant with death and refuge in a lie.

Egypt was a superpower. She represented the best of human power and wisdom. But human power and wisdom can't stand in the face of God's judgment. So Isaiah turns all their confident claims upside down:

> *"I will make justice the measuring line*
> *and righteousness the plumb-line;*
> *hail will sweep away your refuge, the lie,*
> *and water will overflow your hiding-place.*
> *Your covenant with death will be annulled;*
> *your agreement with the realm of the dead*
> *will not stand.*
> *When the overwhelming scourge sweeps by,*
> *you will be beaten down by it."*
>
> (Isaiah 28 v 17-18)

As the flood of God's judgment sweeps across the earth, only one thing stands firm:

> *"See, I lay a stone in Zion, a tested stone,*
> *a precious cornerstone for a sure foundation;*
> *the one who relies on it*
> *will never be stricken with panic." (Isaiah 28 v 16)*

Ultimately the only cornerstone and sure foundation is Jesus (1 Peter 2 v 4, 6).

Perhaps Jesus had Isaiah's words in mind when he told a story of two men each building a house. One builds on the sand. When the storm comes his house soon crumbles. The other builds on the rock and his house stands firm. The man who built on the rock, says Jesus, represents "everyone who hears these words of mine and puts them into practice" (Matthew 7 v 24-27).

What are *you* doing to ensure you regularly hear the words of Jesus? What are you doing to put them into practice?

Meditate

Lord, I was blind: I could not see
In thy marred visage any grace.
But now the beauty of thy face
In radiant vision dawns on me.

Lord, I was deaf: I could not hear
The thrilling music of thy voice.
But now I hear thee and rejoice,
And all thine uttered words are dear.

William T. Matson (1833-1899)

SATURDAY

*Who has believed our message and to whom
has the arm of the* LORD *been revealed?
(Isaiah 53 v 1)*

More times than I can remember, I've stretched out
my arm to rescue a toy before it got trodden on.
That's the image Isaiah uses to picture God's salvation.
In chapters 51 and 52, three calls to *listen up* (51 v 1,
4, 7) are followed by three calls to *wake up* (51 v 9, 17;
52 v 1). Numbers two and three are calls to Jerusalem
to wake up to God. But the first is a call on God himself: "Awake, awake, arm of the LORD, clothe yourself
with strength" (51 v 9). If God's people are going to be
saved, then God will have to act. "The islands will look
to me and wait in hope for my arm," says God (51 v 5).
And Isaiah responds, "Awake, awake, arm of the LORD."
God's arm represents his intervening power in history.
God's arm reaches down from heaven to rescue his people before they're trodden into the dust of death.

Irenaeus, the second-century church father, said the
Son and the Spirit are "the hands of God". They're the
Persons of the Trinity through whom God acts in history.
Jesus is God's arm, reaching down from heaven into
human history, coming in power to rescue his people.

But there's a problem. When people look at Jesus, they see nothing in him that attracts them (53 v 2). Isaiah 53 begins, "Who has believed our message and to whom has the arm of the LORD been revealed?"

One of the key features of Hebrew poetry is parallelism—the same thing is said in parallel ways. This couplet is an example. How is the arm of the LORD revealed? Through the message of God's people. How do people believe in the message? Through the arm of the LORD. God's saving power comes through his word. God's word comes in his saving power.

Isaiah's complaint is that few people have believed his message. Instead, we despise and reject Jesus. Isaiah includes himself in this. Or at least he *used* too. For when Isaiah speaks of "we" in these lines, he uses the past tense. We *used* to find no beauty in Jesus to attract us. But not anymore. Something has changed.

This change is possible because the message comes in the power of the Spirit. Jesus is God's arm, reaching into our history to save his people. And the Spirit is God's other arm, reaching into our hearts to open our eyes to the message of Jesus. Martin Luther says, "To believe that Christ, so exceedingly repulsive and killed between robbers, is the Saviour … that is the work of the Holy Spirit."

This is a great comfort for us as *hearers* of God's message. Whenever we hear God's word, the arm of the Lord is reaching down to us with saving power, comforting power, reviving power, transforming power. Jesus "holds out his arms to receive us," says John Calvin, "as often as the gospel is preached to us".

But this truth is also a comfort to us as *speakers*. For this message has become "*our* message" (v 1). When we speak of Christ, the arm of the Lord is laid bare. God rolls his sleeves up and gets stuck into this world. He reaches down in the power of the Spirit to change hearts and lives.

Meditate

Man of sorrows! What a name
For the Son of God, who came
Ruined sinners to reclaim:
Hallelujah, what a Saviour!

Bearing shame and scoffing rude,
In my place condemned he stood,
Sealed my pardon with his blood:
Hallelujah, what a Saviour!

Guilty, vile, and helpless, we;
Spotless Lamb of God was he.
Full atonement, can it be?
Hallelujah, what a Saviour!

Lifted up was he to die.
"It is finished" was his cry.
Now in heaven exalted high:
Hallelujah, what a Saviour!

When he comes, our glorious King,
All his ransomed home to bring,
Then anew this song we'll sing:
Hallelujah, what a Saviour!

Philip Paul Bliss (1838-1876)

THE THIRD WEEK OF LENT

The Punishment

SUNDAY

Isaiah 53 v 4-6

I wonder what weighs heavily on your conscience. I wonder if there are sins from your past—sins you would rather forget, but which continue to nag away at your memory. Or I wonder if it's the sins of today that trouble you. After all, the sins from the time before you became a Christian were part of your old life, committed when you knew nothing of God's grace. But now you've been born anew. Now your sins are sins against divine love.

Maybe you've been a Christian many years and yet feel how little progress you've made. Or maybe you're beginning to realise how deep down your sin goes. It's not just the wrong things you do; you've discovered the good things you do are all mixed up with pride and self-ishness. Our culture tells us we're basically good—that we're good people who sometimes slip up. But that does little to alleviate the guilt, the shame and the fear.

But the real problem is not how we feel about sin. Our big problem is how *God* feels about our sin. Isaiah keeps calling him "the Holy One of Israel". When Isaiah saw God in his glory, high and exalted, and heard the angels cry, "Holy, holy, holy", he said, "I am ruined" (6 v 5). Left to ourselves, that is our plight and our future: *ruin*.

But we are not left to ourselves.

Pray

Pray through the reading by taking a phrase or two at a time. Each time identify…
- *something to praise God for*
- *something to confess*
- *something to turn into a request*

MONDAY

Surely he took up our pain and bore our suffering.
(Isaiah 53 v 4)

On 23rd March 2018 a gunman stormed a supermarket in the small town of Trèbes in France. He killed two people before taking others hostage. The police managed to rescue some of the people, but the gunman seized a woman, holding her as a human shield. At this point a local policeman, Lt Col Arnaud Beltrame, volunteered to take her place. In the process he placed his mobile phone on a table with an open line so his comrades could follow what was happening. It was on this line that police heard gunfire. They stormed the building, but Lt Col Beltrame had already been shot. He died the following day from his wounds. He swapped places with the woman and as a result gave his life for her.

This story of heroism helps us begin to glimpse the self-sacrifice of Christ. We wonder at it all the more when we appreciate that, whereas the woman at the supermarket was an innocent bystander, who didn't deserve what happened to her, Jesus chose to die for people who are far from innocent and who deserve to be punished. He chose to die in our place—the place of sinners—so that we can go free.

We rightly praise Lt Col Beltrame as a hero, recognising that he did something few others would do. But what the Lord Jesus did for us shows he is a far greater hero. How much more will we want to praise him for his sacrifice.

Look at the pronouns in Isaiah 53 v 4-6, and the central idea quickly becomes clear: *he* took up—*our* pain; *he* bore—*our* suffering; *he* was pierced—for *our* transgressions; *he* was crushed—for *our* iniquities; on *him*—*our* punishment. "These words, OUR, US, FOR US," said Martin Luther, "should be written in gold letters".

Our pain, suffering, transgressions, iniquities and punishment are all transferred to Jesus. And in exchange we receive peace and healing (v 5). He gets what we deserve; we get what he deserves. It's as if we've been struggling under a heavy load, and Jesus has come, lifted the burden from us and carried it himself. Except that this load is one that ultimately crushes whoever bears it.

Verses 4-6 form the central section of Isaiah's poem—the centrepiece, the fulcrum, the crux. But the act it describes is also the centrepiece of the Bible story, of the whole course of human history. Everything turns on an amazing act of substitution. Here's Martin Luther again: "Note the wonderful exchange: one sins, another pays the penalty; one deserves peace, the other has it … This is the supreme and chief article of faith, that our sins, placed on Christ, are not ours; again, that the peace is not Christ's but ours. Once this foundation is established, everything that is built upon it will be well."

How did Isaiah see this? Perhaps he saw the cross through a direct, Spirit-given vision. Or perhaps he recognised the logic of substitution throughout the Bible story. Perhaps it was a bit of both. Substitution didn't come out of the blue. Isaiah had precedents, pictures and parallels to connect it to.

Substitution was there at the beginning when God made clothes for Adam and Eve out of animal skin (Genesis 3 v 21). An animal died to cover our shame. It was there when Abraham was about to kill Isaac, but an angel told him to kill a ram "instead of his son" (Genesis 22 v 13). It was there in the first Passover, when God killed every firstborn child, but passed over Hebrew homes with blood daubed on their lintels (Exodus 11 – 13). The Passover lamb died in our place. It was there in the sacrifices of Israel, as day after day the price of sin was paid in blood, but not our blood. When Isaiah says the servant "*bore*" the sin of many, it's the same word that was used to describe the scapegoat on the Day of Atonement. One animal died in our place; the other "carried" or *bore* the sin of the people away over the horizon (Leviticus 16 v 22).

And so Isaiah realised that at the heart of history would be a great act of substitution. It would be an act so horrible we would turn away and hide our faces (Isaiah 53 v 3). People still turn away, even though the blood has long gone. They can't accept that divine salvation is so brutal and bloody. But this is how deep our sin is and it's how deep God's love goes. People think a bit of moral reform or a dose of religion can cure the problem and that the cross is there simply to inspire us. But "the wages of sin is death" and so something has to die (Romans 6 v 23). And Jesus offers to swap with us. He has died in your place. This is our only hope. But it is a great and certain hope. For Jesus cried on the cross, "It is finished". The price is paid. So for us salvation is free. Who might need you to share this wonderful truth with them right now?

Meditate

How then could God express simultaneously
his holiness in judgment and his love in pardon?
Only by providing a divine substitute for the sinner,
so that the substitute would receive the judgment
and the sinner the pardon.

At the cross in holy love
God through Christ paid the full penalty
of our disobedience himself.
He bore the judgment we deserve
in order to bring us the forgiveness we do not deserve.
On the cross divine mercy and justice
were equally expressed and eternally reconciled.

John Stott (1921-2011)

TUESDAY

Yet we considered him punished by God,
stricken by him, and afflicted.
But he was pierced for our transgressions,
he was crushed for our iniquities.
(Isaiah 53 v 4-5)

I magine seeing a woman's body lying in the street. The contents of her handbag are strewn across the road and a wound from her head is staining the pavement red. A man stands over her, his hands covered in blood. What's happening? You might well assume he's just attacked her. But take a second look. Further up the street a young man is running away. Meanwhile the first man is phoning for an ambulance. We've completely misread the scene. He's not her attacker; he's her saviour. He stepped in to stop her assailant and now he's making sure she gets the medical care she needs.

Imagine seeing Jesus on the cross. Here's a man being punished by God. That much is clear. Yet we've completely misread the scene. For we conclude the servant is being punished because he's guilty. But no, this is not his own guilt. All is not what it seems.

Much of the language in these verses is legal language. "Transgressions" is not simply another general term for sin. It means breaking a law—in this case God's law. Jesus was "punished by God". It's only modern people who look on from 2,000 years away and think the cross was not an act of punishment. The darkened skies and the cry of abandonment made it abundantly clear that this was an act of divine judgment. But Jesus was not being punished for his own crimes. He died bearing the punishment we deserve. He substituted himself for us so he could receive judgment in our place. The theological term for this is "penal substitution"—that's "penal" as in "penalty". It means paying the penalty of sin in our place.

God is a holy God. A sinful person coming into his presence would be like putting tissue paper into a fire— they would be instantly consumed. God is a just God. He must do right. And that includes punishing sin. But God is also a loving God. He is determined to save a people who will be his people. He delights to be merciful.

And God's attributes can't be played off one against the other. He can't stop being holy so he can be merciful. He can't deny his justice for the sake of his love. He is I AM—always the same, always true to himself, always complete in all dimensions of his character. Out of this internal moral consistency, the plan of salvation was born. God will show love and mercy to his people in a way that is entirely consistent with his holiness and justice. And at the heart of that plan is the cross: Jesus bearing our punishment so justice is done; Jesus bearing our punishment so we can walk free.

Isaiah says, "The LORD has laid on him the iniquity of us all" (v 6). The word "laid" literally means "meets". All our sins meet in Jesus. It's as if God focuses down his anger against sin into one intense focal point. And there, at the cross, Jesus absorbed God's judgment against sin to the full. As a result, there is nothing left to pay.

So now the justice of God, which once was our greatest threat, becomes our ally. For justice cannot and will not demand a double payment. God will not make us pay what Christ has already paid in full. The justice of God is no longer a threat. In fact, now we can appeal to God's justice.

It might seem that Jesus is the reluctant victim in this arrangement. But Jesus is not separate from God. God is three Persons with *one* divine being. At the cross God is not judging another. The Father is judging one who is one being with himself. God is both Judge and judged. Father and Son are in perfect agreement, enacting an eternal covenant to redeem God's people.

Meditate

From whence this fear and unbelief,
If God, my Father, put to grief
His spotless Son for me?
Can he, the righteous Judge of men,
Condemn me for that debt of sin
Which, Lord, was charged to thee?

Complete atonement thou hast made,
And to the utmost farthing paid
Whate'er thy people owed;
How, then, can wrath on me take place,

If sheltered in God's righteousness
And sprinkled by thy blood?

If thou hast my discharge procured,
And freely in my place endured
The whole of wrath divine;
Payment God will not twice demand,
First at my bleeding Surety's hand,
And then again at mine.

Turn then, my soul, unto thy rest;
The merits of thy great High Priest
Speak peace and liberty.
Trust in his efficacious blood,
Nor fear thy banishment from God,
Since Jesus died for thee.

Augustus Montague Toplady (1740-1778)

WEDNESDAY

But he was pierced for our transgressions,
he was crushed for our iniquities.
(Isaiah 53 v 5)

Do you do enough evangelism? It's a cheap shot. Most of us all too readily feel pangs of guilt when we think about evangelism. So maybe we should think about something else…

In Isaiah 9 – 10, the nation of Israel thinks it can rebuild without God's help, but it's going to be devoured (9 v 8-12). So Isaiah says, "Yet for all this, *his anger is not turned away*, his hand is still upraised" (9 v 12). The word "upraised" is the word that's used in the story of the exodus to describe God's arm being "outstretched" against Egypt (Exodus 6 v 6). Isaiah says there's going to be a new exodus, but this time God's hand is not stretched out *for* Israel, but *against* Israel.

- God will take away their leaders and prophets because everyone is ungodly (Isaiah 9 v 13-17). But then Isaiah says, "Yet for all this, *his anger is not turned away*, his hand is still upraised" (9 v 17).

- God's judgment is likened to a fire (9 v 18-21). But then Isaiah again says, "Yet for all this, *his anger is not turned away*, his hand is still upraised" (9 v 21).

- Isaiah says that, because of their injustice, there will be nowhere to hide when God judges (10 v 1-4). But guess what! Isaiah again says, "Yet for all this, *his anger is not turned away*, his hand is still upraised" (10 v 4).

- And if Isaiah were here today, he would look across the world, across history; he would look over your life and into your heart, and he would say, "*His anger is not turned away*, his hand is still upraised".

- So perhaps you try so hard to please God, to please other people, to prove yourself. Yet no matter how hard you try, you always seem to fall short. And *his anger is not turned away*.

- Or you try to make amends. You fill your life with activity—you come to church, say your prayers, share your faith. Or maybe you self-harm, punishing yourself for your wrongdoing. But still it never feels enough. For *his anger is not turned away*.

But then Isaiah 12 begins, "In that day you will say: 'I will praise you, LORD. Although you were angry with me, *your anger has turned away* and you have comforted me" (12 v 1). Four times Isaiah has said, "His anger is not turned away" (9 v 12, 17, 21; 10 v 4). But *now* he says, "Your anger *has* turned away". And that's because when Jesus the Servant came, "he was pierced for our transgressions, he was crushed for our iniquities" (53 v 5).

"The LORD himself," says 12 v 2, "he has become my salvation". Salvation is not simply something God *does*. Salvation has become something God *is*. God in the person of Jesus has become the sacrifice. God's anger has fallen, but he turned it away from us and directed it onto himself in the person of Jesus.

Read the rest of Isaiah 12 and notice how Isaiah aligns the commands: "Give praise", "proclaim", "make known", "proclaim", "sing", "let this be known", "shout aloud", "sing for joy"? Our evangelism is so often done out of a sense of guilt. But there's no guilt here. Our guilt was all taken away in 12 v 1. Isaiah's call to mission is fuelled by *joy* (12 v 3, 6). Is it worship or is it evangelism? The two have merged!

Perhaps some of us need to spend less time feeling guilty about our meagre evangelism and more time thinking about Jesus. Perhaps we need to spend more time together drawing water from the wells of salvation (12 v 3). We need to rediscover our enthusiasm for Jesus. It's a bit like shaking a bottle of champagne. When an opportunity comes to tell someone about Jesus... *Psssh!* We fizz with excitement for Jesus.

Meditate

Hail, thou once despisèd Jesus!
Hail, thou Galilean King!
Thou didst suffer to release us;
Thou didst free salvation bring.
Hail, thou universal Saviour,
Who hast borne our sin and shame!
By thy merits we find favour;
Life is given through thy name.

Paschal Lamb, by God appointed,
All our sins on thee were laid.
By almighty love anointed,
Thou hast full atonement made.
Every sin may be forgiven
Through the virtue of thy blood;
Opened is the gate of heaven,
Reconciled are we with God.

John Bakewell (1721-1819)

THURSDAY

He was crushed for our iniquities.
(Isaiah 53 v 5)

Today I want us to listen to a piece of music in five movements.

The first movement begins with a bang—with an explosion of sound as the triumphant melody soars up high. (If you're into classical music, then think of the moment the choir first bursts into song in Handel's coronation anthem "Zadok the Priest".) Isaiah sees a vision of God. "In the year that King Uzziah died," he says in 6 v 1, "I saw the Lord, high and exalted, seated on a throne; and the train of his robe filled the temple". This song starts on a high—quite literally. It starts with God, "high and exalted". The angels declare that he is holy. The glory of God is so magnificent that it fills the temple. When God is present, there is no room left for anything other than his glory.

The second movement brings us to Isaiah's song in chapters 52 – 53, and we're still on a high. God himself takes up the tune. It's the same melody, the same high notes, but this time it's about Jesus the Servant. "See, my servant … he will be raised and lifted up and highly exalted" (52 v 13). The glory of God in his heavenly temple will be matched by the glory of the Servant on earth.

The third movement comes in Isaiah 57 v 15, and again it's God who is singing. Again he's described as "the high and exalted One". Again his name is holy. This is the Lord whom Isaiah saw in the first movement "high and exalted" in his temple. But what the Lord sings is extraordinary:

> *For this is what the high and exalted One says—*
> *   he who lives for ever, whose name is holy:*
> *"I live in a high and holy place,*
> *   but also with the one who is contrite and lowly in*
> *spirit, to revive the spirit of the lowly*
> *   and to revive the heart of the contrite."*
>
> *(Isaiah 57 v 15)*

The notes come plunging down the scale. We move from "a high and holy place" to the "contrite and lowly in spirit". The song has moved from God's Servant (Jesus) to God's servants (us). God promises to live among his people—among those who feel the weight of their sin.

For the fourth movement we go back to the song of Isaiah 53. The word "contrite" in 57 v 15 literally means "crushed" or even "pulverised". It's used to describe Jesus in Isaiah 53: "He was crushed for our iniquities" (v 5) and "it was the LORD's will to crush him" (v 10). Here the music shifts into a minor key. (Think of the "Symphony of Sorrowful Songs" by the Polish composer Henryk Górecki.) Here Jesus the Servant is pulverised on the cross. He is crushed by God's judgment. It bears down on him until he breaks under its weight.

But he is crushed for *our* iniquities. He is broken in *our* place. God may allow us to feel abandoned, but he never truly abandons us. Only Christ, alone of all God's people, was truly abandoned—and he was abandoned on our behalf.

For the finale, we return to Isaiah 57 v 15, but this time we carry the tune we have learnt from chapter 53, except that now it's transposed into a major key. It has transformed into a song of hope and joy. (Think Beethoven's "Ode to Joy".) The promise that God, the high and exalted one, will live with the contrite or crushed has become a promise that God will live with those who are in Christ. Christ was crushed so we can be lifted up—up into the presence of God.

The way down is the way up. We ascend to God by lowering ourselves, humbling ourselves, admitting our desperate need for Jesus. We let go of any merits we may think we have and cling resolutely to Christ's merits. "Humble yourselves, therefore, under God's mighty hand, that he may lift you up in due time" (1 Peter 5 v 6).

Meditate

By weakness and defeat
He won the glorious crown;
Trod all his foes beneath His feet
By being trodden down.

He hell in hell laid low;
Made sin, he sin o'erthrew;
Bowed to the grave, destroyed it so,
And death, by dying, slew.

Samuel W. Gandy (1780-1851)

FRIDAY

The punishment that brought us peace was on him ...
We all, like sheep, have gone astray,
each of us has turned to our own way.
(Isaiah 53 v 5-6)

I don't know if you've ever tried gathering sheep. Maybe you've come across a stray sheep in a lane or along a path. The sheep instinctively runs away from you, even though that means its heading towards danger. You try to steer it back to safety, but any move you make towards it drives it further away. Isaiah says *we* are like sheep.

The cross, he says, has "brought us peace" (v 5). Isaiah is not talking about an inner calm—though that may be one of the fruits of the peace of which he speaks. Nor is he talking about the end of war—though that, too, will come when Jesus reigns on earth. Isaiah is talking about reconciliation with God. Sin is an act of rebellion. We have become God's enemies. But Christ has made peace between humanity and God: "the punishment that brought us peace was on him" (v 5).

Jesus brings peace by changing the attitude of both sides of this war. He turns God's hostility towards us into God's favour by removing our sin. It's not that God the Father is reluctant to accept us and has to be won over by Jesus. This plan starts with the Father's love. He is the great initiator. But for reconciliation to take place, Jesus had to remove God's judgment against us by absorbing it in his own body. Now the way is clear for God to forgive us and bless us.

But Jesus also transforms *our attitude* towards God. Returning to God begins with an act of repentance. And so it is that the Book of Common Prayer begins the daily prayer of confession with words that echo verse 6: "Almighty and most merciful Father, we have erred, and strayed from thy ways like lost sheep". Isaiah has spoken of our sin as an act of law-breaking ("transgressions"), as an act of evil ("iniquity"), and as an illness that infects our souls ("wounds" that need healing). Now he describes it as being lost: "We all, like sheep, have gone astray" (v 6). We have wandered away from God and are refusing to be led home.

You will only truly come back to God once you've grasped by faith that God welcomes you as a loving Father. No one runs into the arms of a harsh judge. But we come to God in confidence because of Christ. The wounds of Christ welcome us home. "'He himself bore our sins' in his body on the cross, so that we might die to sins and live for righteousness; 'by his wounds you have been healed.' For 'you were like sheep going astray,' but now you have returned to the Shepherd and Overseer of your souls" (1 Peter 2 v 24-25).

Let me paraphrase how Martin Luther applies these words:

Here's what you should do when you feel your sins weighing on your conscience. Don't be afraid. Instead, by faith, take them off yourself and place them on Christ. For this text says, "He has borne our iniquities". It's clear that we need to entrust our sins to Christ. If you think your sins still belong to you, then this thought doesn't come from God but from Satan because it is contrary to God's word. For in God's word, God places your sins on Christ. So here's what you should say to yourself. "I see my sins on Christ. So my sin is no longer mine. It belongs to another. For I see it there on Christ." It's a great thing to be able to say, "My sin is not my own any more … My sins have been transferred to Christ and now they are his responsibility."

Meditate

*The Maker of man was made man,
that the Ruler of the stars might suck at the breast;
that the Bread might hunger;
the Fountain thirst;
the Light sleep;
the Way be wearied by the journey;
the Truth be accused by false witnesses;
the Judge of the living and the dead
be judged by a mortal judge;
the Chastener be chastened with whips;
the Vine be crowned with thorns;
the Foundation be hung upon the tree;
Strength be made weak;
Health be wounded;*

Life die.
He was made man
to suffer these and suchlike, undeserved things,
that he might free the undeserving,
for neither did he deserve any evil,
who for our sakes endured so many evils,
nor were we deserving of anything good,
who through him received such good.

Augustine (354-430)

SATURDAY

And by his wounds we are healed.
(Isaiah 53 v 5)

Matthew tells us how a leper comes to Jesus and says, "Lord, if you are willing, you can make me clean". The leper is healed. Then a centurion comes on behalf of his servant. Jesus offers to come home to see the sick man. But the centurion demurs, counting himself unworthy to entertain Jesus. Instead he says, "Just say the word, and my servant will be healed". "Go!" says Jesus. "Let it be done just as you believed it would." In that very moment, the servant is cured. Finally, Jesus goes to Peter's home, where he finds Peter's mother-in-law with a high fever. With a touch,

Jesus heals her. That evening Jesus heals many more demon-possessed and sick people (Matthew 8 v 1-16).

Matthew sums up these stories with a quote from Isaiah 53 v 4: "This was to fulfil what was spoken through the prophet Isaiah: 'He took up our infirmities and bore our diseases'" (Matthew 8 v 17).

What's the lesson we're supposed to draw? Is it that we can expect Jesus to heal our illnesses? Will my cold clear up with a prayer? Will my tumour disappear? Perhaps. But that's not the message Matthew wants us to draw. The quote from Isaiah, as we've seen, is all about Jesus being punished in our place. "He was pierced for our transgressions, he was crushed for our iniquities." It's an odd quote to bring up if this is only about Jesus healing people. No—as we've seen, the quote from Isaiah tells us that Jesus was punished in our place for *our sin*.

That's the point: there was no sickness in the world before the arrival of sin. It was only when humanity rebelled against God that this earth—including our bodies—came under God's curse. Sickness is a sign of sin. That's not normally true on a case-by-case basis. Jesus makes that very clear (John 9). It's not normally the case that my cold is a judgment against a lie I told a few days ago, or that your tumour is a result of a specific sin from your past (though occasionally God uses sickness to warn us from specific sin; for example, 1 Corinthians 11 v 27-32).

But sickness *in general* is the result of sin *in general*. Humanity sinned; as a result, sickness and death have become part of our world.

Jesus came not simply to deal with the symptoms of sin—like sickness. He came to deal with the root problem: sin itself and God's judgment against sin. When Isaiah says that Jesus "took up our pain and bore our suffering", he's not simply saying that Jesus sometimes fell ill like us. He's saying Jesus tackled the root of sickness by being "pierced for our transgressions". Theodoret, one of the early church fathers, said in the fifth century, "This is a new and strange way of healing: the physician undergoes the operation and the patient obtains the healing".

But, by tackling the problem at its source, Jesus has also tackled the symptoms. He rose again as the promise and beginning of a new world: a world without sickness where there will be "no more death or mourning or crying or pain" (Revelation 21 v 4). That world is coming. And it was anticipated in the ministry of Jesus. Every miracle that Jesus performed was a sign of the coming world.

We're not there yet. And so today some of us are ill and all of us are moving towards death. But here's the promise of Isaiah 53 and Matthew 8: *every Christian will be healed*. Perhaps in this life. Certainly in the life to come. We will all end up sharing the resurrection life of Jesus. We will all receive a new body in a new world.

In the meantime, God is healing the wounds of our souls. That sin that weighs heavily on your conscience—you can let Christ lift it from you. That sin that nags away at your memory—God chooses not to remember it. The guilt and shame you hide in your heart are cleansed by the wounds of Christ. What about the sins of today—not just the wrong you do but also the good you don't do? Just as your sin continues, so does the work of Christ. "Because Jesus lives for ever, he has a permanent priesthood," says Hebrews 7 v 24-25. "Therefore he is able to save completely those who come to God through him."

What about the deep-down sin that taints everything you do? Look to the cross and discover afresh that God's love is deeper.

Meditate

You know some foul diseases pass from us
by the transmission of the infection to others.
Christ was infected, as it were, by our corruptions,
that we might be free.

We, that were dead in sins, are now dead to sin,
the vigour and strength of sin
being extinguished by virtue
derived from Christ's bearing of them,
whereby the soul is restored to health again ...

The love of Christ is seen in that
he would not only take away the guilt of sins,
but take it into his own person.
Here is the lowest condescension,
and so the highest expression of love,
that he was "made sin".

Thomas Manton (1620–1677)

THE FOURTH WEEK OF LENT

The

Silence

SUNDAY

Isaiah 53 v 7-9

On September 11th 1973 General Augusto Pinochet seized power in Chile in a military coup. In the following years, he oversaw a regime that imprisoned around 80,000 opponents. Thousands were tortured. Over 3,000 people simply disappeared.

Fifteen years later, I was sitting at home watching the television when the newsreader announced that Pinochet had been arrested on a visit to London. As the news broke, I cheered. Audibly. I remember it well because I took myself by surprise.

It was a visceral reminder of how much we long for justice. I had no personal connection to Pinochet's victims. I've never visited Chile. Yet still I reacted to his arrest with pleasure. (Pinochet was eventually allowed to return to Chile on health grounds where, as legal arguments rumbled on, he died under house arrest.)

Our newspapers are full of exposés of injustice—from the mistakes of petty bureaucrats to the crimes of brutal dictators. We complain when we're wronged. We protest when we're abused. And we tell our stories with every expectation that other people will share our outrage.

But the servant—Jesus the Servant—is silent.

Pray

Pray through the reading by taking a phrase or two at a time. Each time identify...
- *something to praise God for*
- *something to confess*
- *something to turn into a request*

MONDAY

He was oppressed and afflicted.
(Isaiah 53 v 7)

Out of the corner of his eye, Moses saw flames. Nothing unusual about that—not out here in the desert. So he went back to counting sheep. A few minutes later, though, he looked up and saw the bush was still burning—burning, but not being consumed. Time to investigate this strange sight.

Stranger still was to come. For God spoke Moses' name from the bush and told him to take off his sandals because this was holy ground. It would prove to be the defining moment of Moses' life. For this was the moment in which God called Moses to lead his people out of slavery in Egypt. And this "exodus" from slavery would prove to be the defining moment in the nation's life. This event, more than any other, would shape the identity of the people of Israel and their understanding of God.

This is how God begins his conversation with Moses at the burning bush: "I have indeed seen the misery of my people in Egypt. I have heard them crying out because of their slave drivers, and I am concerned about their suffering" (Exodus 3 v 7).

Sound familiar? The word "oppressed" in Isaiah 53 v 7 is the word translated "slave drivers" in Exodus 3 v 7; the servant is "oppressed" just as the Israelites were oppressed by their slave drivers. And the word "afflicted" in Isaiah 53 v 7 is related to the word "misery" in Exodus 3 v 7. And the word "suffering" in Exodus 3 v 7 is the used of the servant in Isaiah 53 v 3-4.

Putting these together, we can see that when Jesus was hanging on the cross, he experienced what the Israelites experienced in Egypt. Could this be the beginning of another exodus? Could this be another defining moment?

Isaiah's answer is an emphatic *Yes*. Again and again, he speaks of God's coming rescue in language that recalls the exodus. Take, for example, Isaiah 43. Look out for the parting of the Red Sea and the drowning of the Egyptian army (the story told in Exodus 14):

This is what the LORD says—
   he who made a way through the sea,
   a path through the mighty waters,
who drew out the chariots and horses,
   the army and reinforcements together,
and they lay there, never to rise again,
   extinguished, snuffed out like a wick:

"Forget the former things;
  do not dwell on the past.
See, I am doing a new thing!"

(*Isaiah 43 v 16-19*)

You remember the exodus? says God. *Well, now forget about it. That's history. I'm going to do it again. But this time it will be bigger and better. This time I'll tackle the real slavery that ensnares humanity—the slavery to sin. And I'll defeat the final enemy—death.*

When the true glory of Jesus was momentarily revealed in what we call the transfiguration, Moses and Elijah appeared alongside him. Luke says they "appeared in glorious splendour, talking with Jesus" (Luke 9 v 30). Now that's a conversation I wish I had overheard. Luke summarises its content with just one word: *exodus*. "They spoke," he says in 9 v 31, "about his departure, which he was about to bring to fulfilment at Jerusalem." The word "departure" is literally "exodus".

What wonderful truth do all these repeated words show us? They show that the cross and resurrection in Jerusalem are the new exodus. This is the moment when all Isaiah's hopes are realised. This is *our* moment of liberation. This is *our* exodus.

Meditate

In our sickness we need a Saviour,
in our wanderings a guide,
in our blindness someone to show us the light,
in our thirst the fountain of living water

that quenches for ever the thirst of those
who drink from it.
We dead people need life,
we sheep need a shepherd,
we children need a teacher,
the whole world needs Jesus!

Clement of Alexandria (c. 150 – c. 215)

TUESDAY

He was led like a lamb to the slaughter.
(Isaiah 53 v 7)

At the heart of the story of the exodus is the night of Passover, the last of the ten plagues. Before this, God turned the rivers of Egypt red with blood to urge Pharaoh to liberate God's people, Israel. But Pharaoh refused. There was no way he was going to be told what to do. He believed he was the most powerful man in the world, with the gods of Egypt on his side. So next the Lord God sent plagues of frogs, gnats and flies. Still Pharaoh did not budge. Nine plagues later, and still Pharaoh was refusing to let God's people go free. And so this great confrontation came to its inevitable climax. In a tenth and final plague, God would strike down every firstborn son—human and animal—throughout the land of Egypt.

The people of Israel were in the firing line just as much as the people of Egypt. After all, they had no moral superiority. They deserved judgment just as much as the next family. But God in his grace provided a way of escape. Each family had to kill a lamb and daub its blood over the lintels of their home. Wherever God saw the blood, he would "pass over" that house. When morning dawned the next day, something had died in every home in Egypt: either a lamb or a child. Among God's people, the lamb had died in the place of the child.

If we were judging by Isaiah 53 v 7 alone, then we might conclude that Isaiah speaks of a lamb simply to illustrate the servant's patience. After all, Isaiah is concerned in this verse not just with lambs being slaughtered, but also with the shearing of sheep. But verse 7 doesn't stand alone. As we saw yesterday, Isaiah has just used the language of the exodus to describe the plight of Jesus the Servant, and he has been alluding to a new exodus throughout his ministry. And now in this key section, it is perhaps inevitable that he speaks of a new Passover lamb.

How will the new exodus be achieved? In the same way as the first exodus—through a lamb substituted in the place of the people.

Perhaps Isaiah glimpsed what the writer of Hebrews saw so clearly: "It is impossible for the blood of bulls and goats to take away sins" (Hebrews 10 v 4).

Perhaps Isaiah glimpsed what John the Baptist saw in flesh and blood when he saw Jesus coming towards him and declared, "Look, the Lamb of God, who takes away the sin of the world!" (John 1 v 29).

Perhaps Isaiah glimpsed what Peter understood only after it was all done and dusted. In the moment of Jesus' arrest, Peter denied ever knowing Jesus. Only later did he recognise what had happened:

> *For you know that it was not with perishable things such as silver or gold that you were redeemed from the empty way of life handed down to you from your ancestors, but with the precious blood of Christ, a lamb without blemish or defect.* (1 Peter 1 v 18-19)

Sometimes our old, empty way of life seems very attractive. Just as the people of Israel sometimes wanted to return to Egypt, sometimes we want to go back to our sin. In those moments of temptation, remember the price of our salvation: we were bought with the precious blood of Christ.

When do you find this hardest to live out? How will you help yourself to stand firm the next time you are tempted to return to your old way of life?

Meditate

Christ, our Passover lamb, has been sacrificed.
Therefore let us keep the Festival,
not with the old bread leavened with
malice and wickedness,
but with the unleavened bread of sincerity and truth.

1 Corinthians 5 v 7-8

WEDNESDAY

He was oppressed and afflicted,
yet he did not open his mouth;
he was led like a lamb to the slaughter,
and as a sheep before its shearers is silent,
so he did not open his mouth. (Isaiah 53 v 7)

What do we usually do when threatened? Fight or flight. Shout or sprint. Hit or hide.

But not the Servant. The big emphasis in these verses of the song is on the *silence* of the lamb. This section begins and ends with a reference to his mouth: "he did not open his mouth" (v 7); "nor was any deceit in his mouth" (v 9). We're given a good reason why he might have shouted: he was oppressed. But, no, "he did not open his mouth". Then we're given parallels. Just like a lamb going to the slaughter or a sheep to the shearer, "so he did not open his mouth"—the same words.

The point Isaiah wants to make is that Jesus the Servant goes to his death of his own accord. His silence speaks eloquently of his willingness. His apparent passivity is actually a powerful sign of his determination to face death.

What do people normally do when they're accused? They raise their voices in protest. And what do people do when faced with the threat of violence? Fight or flight. They either put up a struggle or they do their best to run away. But not Jesus the Servant.

> *When he was accused by the chief priests and the elders, he gave no answer. Then Pilate asked him, "Don't you hear the testimony they are bringing against you?" But Jesus made no reply, not even to a single charge—to the great amazement of the governor.*
>
> *(Matthew 27 v 12-14)*

Jesus listened to his accusers in silence. He went to his death without a struggle. Why? Because this was the course of action he was determined to pursue. This was the Father's plan for the redemption of his people. Empowered by the Spirit and full of love for his bride, the church, Jesus chose the cross. In the Garden of Gethsemane, he shrank back from the horror of what he must endure. He shrank—but then resolved to go forward.

When the soldiers came to arrest him, Jesus declared, "I am he". It's literally, "I AM"—an echo of God's revelation to Moses in Exodus 3 v 14. It's a phrase Isaiah uses seven times (41 v 4; 43 v 10, 25; 46 v 4; 48 v 12; 51 v 12; 52 v 6). The soldiers drew back and fell to the ground (John 18 v 6). They were encountering the almighty God in human form. The next thing that happened was that Peter pulled out a sword. But Jesus said, "Put your sword away! Shall I not drink the cup the Father has given me?" (John 18 v 11).

This is important. When we talk, as Isaiah does, about God the Father punishing Jesus in our place, it can sound as if Jesus is the reluctant victim. But nothing could be further from the truth. This was a man in command of his destiny—a man who was determined to pay the price of our sin.

So Jesus let himself be taken, tried, whipped, mocked and crucified. Jesus once said, "The reason my Father loves me is that I lay down my life—only to take it up again. No one takes it from me, but I lay it down of my own accord. I have authority to lay it down and authority to take it up again. This command I received from my Father" (John 10 v 17-18).

In the final analysis it wasn't the nails that held him on the cross, or the weapons of the soldiers gathered round its base. In the end, what held Jesus to the cross was love. Love for us. Love for *you*.

Meditate

We usually think the highest expressions of love
involve someone acting out of character
in order to do us good—
as when a stern person is tender
or a cautious person is bold.
So it is that the greatest ever act of self-denial
was when Christ became sin for us.
Oh, work this truth into your hearts
and display it before your faith!

Thomas Manton (1620-1677)

THURSDAY

Though he had done no violence,
nor was any deceit in his mouth.
(Isaiah 53 v 9)

What should we do when our television screens are full of comedians scorning our values or academics making a mockery of our beliefs? What do you do when your boss dumps extra work on you and then berates you for your poor attitude—and all the time you suspect he's got it in for you because of your faith? What should you do when every hour spent with your church family involves a battle with your unbelieving spouse?

It's not hard to hear an echo of these challenges in the exhortations of 1 Peter. These scenarios were familiar to Peter's readers:

- *"It is God's will that by doing good you should silence the ignorant talk of foolish people" (1 Peter 2 v 15).*

- *"Slaves, in reverent fear of God submit yourselves to your masters, not only to those who are good and considerate, but also to those who are harsh" (1 Peter 2 v 18).*

- *"Wives, in the same way submit yourselves to your own husbands so that, if any of them do not believe the word, they may be won over without words by the behaviour of their wives, when they see the purity and reverence of your lives" (1 Peter 3 v 1-2).*

Where does Peter go in order to ground this tough teaching? What's the basis for these exhortations? Answer: Isaiah 53. Peter points to the example of the suffering servant.

> *But how is it to your credit if you receive a beating for doing wrong and endure it? But if you suffer for doing good and you endure it, this is commendable before God. To this you were called, because Christ suffered for you, leaving you an example, that you should follow in his steps.*
>
> *"He committed no sin,
> and no deceit was found in his mouth."*
>
> *When they hurled their insults at him, he did not retaliate; when he suffered, he made no threats. Instead, he entrusted himself to him who judges justly.*
> *(1 Peter 2 v 20-23)*

Jesus the Servant has set an example we should follow. In the process, Peter provides his own take on the servant's silence. It is not that he never speaks. It's not even that he never defends himself. Though there were moments during his trials when Jesus was silent, there were also moments when he spoke up. The point is he never retaliated and he never made threats. He never responded to violence with violence, to violent words with violent words. We can defend ourselves when accused. But our attitude and our actions must not become aggressive.

How can we remain calm in the face of provocation? Like the servant, we can entrust ourselves to him who judges justly (1 Peter 2 v 23). You don't need to retaliate. What difference will that make next time you are wronged? You don't need to make threats. What difference will that make next time you're treated unfairly?

Jesus was silent before his accusers because he knew that what was happening was God's plan, and he knew God would have the last word. And so can we.

Meditate

Brothers and sisters, what are you doing for Jesus?
I charge you by the nail-prints of his hands
—labour for him!
I charge you by his wounded feet
—run to his help!
I charge you by the scar on his side
—give him your heart!
I charge you by that sacred head once pierced with thorns
—yield him your thoughts!
I charge you by the shoulders which bore the scourges
—bend your whole strength to his service!
I charge you by himself
—give him yourself …

Live in his service, and die in his service!
Lay not down your harness,
but work on as long as you shall live.

C. H. Spurgeon (1834-1892)

FRIDAY

As a sheep before its shearers is silent,
so he did not open his mouth.
(Isaiah 53 v 7)

In 1662 John Flavel, then a minister in Dartmouth in Devon, refused to submit to the Act of Uniformity, introduced by King Charles II to roll back Puritan reforms. Flavel lost his job and was banned from the town. So he went underground, slipping into Dartmouth in disguise and preaching to secret gatherings. Ten years later he was allowed to return, but continued to face harassment. Yet Flavel turned down the opportunity to preach in the relative safety of London. House arrest and more restrictions followed. On top of all his public troubles, Flavel was widowed twice.

So when John Flavel spoke about suffering, he knew what he was talking about. Here's his advice (edited and updated) on how we can follow the example of Jesus the Servant and face suffering with patience…

1. Look upwards, when troubles come upon you. Look to the Sovereign Lord, who commissions and sends them to you. Your troubles do not rise out of the dust, but are constructed in heaven (Jeremiah 18 v 11). And in the construction of your afflictions, you may observe much divine wisdom in the choice, measure and timing of your troubles.

2. Look downward, and see what is below you. You are afflicted, and think you cannot bear it. "Oh, there's no trouble like my trouble!" you say. Well, well, cast your mind downward, and see those who lie much lower than you. Or if you think there is no one suffering like you on earth, then you must concede there are many in hell who would be glad to change conditions with you, as bad as you think yours to be.

3. Look inward, and see if you can find reasons for patience there. Can't you find weeds enough there that need winter weather like this to kill them? Doesn't your proud heart need this to humble it? That selfish heart needs such things as these to kill its selfishness. And as your sinful desires call for trouble, so do your graces too. Why do think you the Lord planted faith, humility, patience and so on in your soul? What, were they put there for nothing? Did the Lord intend them to lie sleeping in their drowsy habits? Or were they not planted there in order to be used? And how shall they be used without troubles?

4. Look outward, and see who observes your conduct under trouble. There is hardly any greater pleasure for the wicked than to see your conduct under trouble being just like their own. For in this way they are confirmed in their prejudices against religion, and in their good opinion of themselves. "These Christians," they say, "talk of heaven's glory, but it is all just talk, for it is clear enough that their hopes cannot compensate for even small afflictions". Oh, how you dishonour Christ when you make his enemies think all your religion is empty talk!

5. *Look backward*, and consult the many past experiences of trouble, both your own and those of others. Is this the first difficulty ever you have faced? If so, you have reason to bless God for sparing you so long when others have had days filled with sorrow. But if you have been in trouble before, and the Lord has helped you, then you have good reason to patiently wait for the salvation of God! If he helped you then, can he not do so now?

6. *Look forward*, to the end of your troubles. Our troubles are "light and momentary" (2 Corinthians 4 v 17). What are a few days of sorrows when they are past? Are they not swallowed up like a spoonful of water in the vast ocean of eternity? But even more, look to the *purpose* of your troubles. Are they not achieving for us an eternal glory that far outweighs them all? (v 17) Are you not made sharers in God's holiness by them? (Hebrews 12 v 10)

7. *Look to the right hand*, and see how you are shamed, convicted and silenced by other Christians. It may be you will find some poor Christian who doesn't know where their next meal will come from, and yet they are speaking of the bounty of their God, while you are moaning in the midst of plenty.

8. Look to your left hand. There you may see a company of wicked, graceless wretches, conducting themselves in their troubles too much like you. It's time for you to stop when you see how close you have become to them.

Reader, these considerations will help your soul at such times. But above all, look to the great model of patience, Jesus Christ, and his lamb-like suffering under a trial— sufferings with which yours should not be named on the same day. O how this example should transform you into a meek lamb as well!

Meditate

Father God, I ask you to fill me
with the knowledge of your will
through all the wisdom and understanding
that the Spirit gives,
so that I may live a life worthy of the Lord Jesus
and please him in every way:
bearing fruit in every good work,
growing in the knowledge of God,
being strengthened with all power
according to his glorious might
so that I may have great endurance and patience,
and giving joyful thanks to you, Father,
for you have qualified me to share
in the inheritance of your holy people
in the kingdom of light.

Based on Colossians 1 v 9-12

SATURDAY

By oppression and judgment he was taken away.
Yet who of his generation protested?
For he was cut off from the land of the living;
for the transgression of my people he was punished.
He was assigned a grave with the wicked,
and with the rich in his death.
(Isaiah 53 v 8-9)

In recent years some new phrases have entered our vo-cabulary: *extraordinary rendition, extra-judicial killing, black ops.* They are used when a person disappears, or is imprisoned or even executed without the due process of law.

That's how Isaiah paints the fate of the servant. "By oppression and judgment he was taken away" (v 8). The language implies an unjust act. "Yet who of his generation protested?" No one stood up for him. He was pulled off the streets and bundled away, and no one cared.

And so it was for Jesus. No advocate stood beside him. No journalists investigated his story. The judicial process found Jesus innocent. "The chief priests and the whole Sanhedrin," says Mark 14 v 55, "were looking for evidence against Jesus so that they could put him to death, but they did not find any". "I have found in him no grounds for the death penalty," said Pilate (Luke 23 v 22). And yet Jesus was condemned to death. Pilate, says Luke, "surrendered Jesus to their will" (v 25).

Jesus was condemned and the world was silent. For this is the will of the world. The world only speaks up to shout, "Crucify him!" This is our verdict on Jesus. All of us have in some measure lived our lives as if Jesus doesn't matter, and as if his claim to be Lord is false.

The silence of Jesus speaks powerfully of his willingness to die in our place. Our silence speaks powerfully of our *need* for him to die in our place. His trial proves his innocence, but his trial also demonstrates humanity's guilt. Jesus has surrendered himself to our will, and our will is his death. We push him out of our lives and onto the cross. We have executed Jesus a thousand times over by our refusal to submit to him. What happened 2,000 years ago in Jerusalem was simply the logical conclusion of decisions we make each and every day.

His burial is ambiguous: "He was assigned a grave with the wicked, and with the rich in his death" (Isaiah 53 v 9). In the parallelism of Hebrew poetry, we might expect "wicked" and "rich" to complement one another. But in the original Hebrew, "wicked ones" is plural while the "rich one" is singular. It suggests two distinct parties—a group of wicked people and a single rich man. There would be something dishonourable about Jesus' death, and yet his body would not simply be dumped. Instead, he would be buried in a rich man's grave. What would Isaiah and his contemporaries have made of these words? It's hard to know. How could a condemned man receive a rich man's burial? It only really made sense as the events themselves unfolded. Here's Matthew's account:

As evening approached, there came a rich man from Arimathea, named Joseph, who had himself become a disciple of Jesus. Going to Pilate, he asked for Jesus' body, and Pilate ordered that it be given to him. Joseph took the body, wrapped it in a clean linen cloth, and placed it in his own new tomb that he had cut out of the rock. He rolled a big stone in front of the entrance to the tomb and went away.   (Matthew 27 v 57-60)

Jesus was put to death "with the help of wicked men" (Acts 2 v 23). But because of Joseph of Arimathea, Jesus was buried in a rich man's grave. The word "though" in Isaiah 53 v 9 is normally translated "because". Jesus was not buried in a rich man's grave *despite* having done no violence. He was buried with all due respect *because* he had done no violence. It's a hint that there might be another way of viewing this execution. Somebody cared. His death had not gone unnoticed. What difference will that make to your thoughts and feelings this week?

Meditate

He was tempted as Man, but he conquered as God;
indeed, he bids us be of good cheer
for he has overcome the world.
He hungered, but he fed thousands;
indeed, he is the Bread that gives life,
the bread of heaven.
He thirsted, but he cried,
"If anyone thirsts, let them come to me and drink";
indeed, he promised that fountains should flow
from them who believe.

He was weary, but he is the rest
of those who are weary and heavy-laden.
He prays, but he hears prayer.
He weeps, but he causes tears to cease.
He is sold, and very cheaply,
for it was only for thirty pieces of silver,
but he redeems the world,
and at a great price, for the price was his own blood.

As a sheep he is led to the slaughter,
but he is the Shepherd of Israel,
and now of the whole world as well.
As a Lamb he is silent, but he is the Word.
He is bruised and wounded,
but he heals every disease and every infirmity.
He is lifted up and nailed to the Tree,
but by the Tree of Life he restores us;
indeed, he saves even the robber crucified with him.
He is given vinegar to drink mingled with gall.
Who? He who turned the water into wine,
who is the destroyer of the bitter taste,
who is Sweetness and the altogether lovely One.
He lays down his life, but he has power to take it again,
and the veil is torn,
for the mysterious doors of heaven are opened;
the rocks are cleft, the dead arise.
He dies, but he gives life,
and by his death destroys death.

Gregory of Nazianzus (329-390)

THE FIFTH WEEK OF LENT

The
Spoils

SUNDAY

Isaiah 53 v 10-12

How do you think other people view you? Do they see your virtues or do they see your faults? Do they like you? Perhaps that's a question you avoid thinking too much about.

I don't know if you've had a situation when you've tried to spend time with someone and they've put you off. You're left wondering whether they were genuinely busy or just finding excuses not to hang out with you. So you're reluctant to invite them again. (Perhaps that only happens to me!) What you think other people make of you affects how you relate to them.

What about God? How do you think God views you? Does he want to spend time with you? It's an important question because it will affect how you relate to him. It's a question addressed in Isaiah 53 v 10-12 as we see Jesus the Servant's victory and his relationship with his people.

Pray
Pray through the reading by taking a phrase or two at a time. Each time identify…
- *something to praise God for*
- *something to confess*
- *something to turn into a request*

MONDAY

Yet it was the LORD's will to crush him
and cause him to suffer, and ...
the LORD makes his life an offering for sin.
(Isaiah 53 v 10)

In the Speedwell Mine in the English Peak District is a cavern with a lake. The miners used to think it was bottomless. They dumped their spoil into it and it never filled up. Only once the mine had closed did someone drop a weighted line into it to measure its depths. Rather disappointingly, it turned out that the miners had almost filled it.

Just how deep is the love of God?

Wicked men were involved in the death of Jesus the Servant (v 9). But they were not the only ones to be involved. Indeed, they weren't the primary agents of his death. He died as part of God's will. When we looked at verse 9 last week we quoted Acts 2 v 23, showing that Jesus died "with the help of wicked men". But here's the verse in full: "This man was handed over to you by God's deliberate plan and foreknowledge; and you, with the help of wicked men, put him to death by nailing him to the cross."

Jesus died "by God's deliberate plan and foreknowledge". Describing Jesus as the Passover lamb, Peter says, "He was chosen before the creation of the world, but was revealed in these last times for your sake" (1 Peter 1 v 20). This choice was made before time began. Father, Son and Spirit saw humanity's rebellion and had compassion on our plight. Together they agreed a plan. They made a pact among themselves: an eternal covenant of redemption. At the heart of that plan was the offering of the Son. This would be the supreme revelation of divine love. "The Lamb," says Revelation 13 v 8, "was slain from the creation of the world". The cross was always going to be the centrepiece of history. The universe was constructed as the stage for this act.

The word "offering" in Isaiah 53 v 10 is the technical term for a "guilt offering" (Leviticus 5 v 14-19; 6 v 6-7; 7 v 1-10). It made provision for anyone sinning against "the LORD's holy things" (Leviticus 5 v 15). For the Israelites, that had a ritual meaning. But their rituals illustrated the true nature of sin. *We sin against God whenever we fail to live in a way consistent with his holiness.* And we know that includes mistreating people made in his image, since the guilt offering also covered offences against a neighbour (6 v 1-3).

The guilt offering itself involved both the sacrifice of an animal and a payment of "restitution" (5 v 16-19; 6 v 4-7). Old Testament scholar Gordon Wenham calls it "the reparation offering or the compensation offering". It contains both the idea of "substitutionary atonement—of the ram dying in the sinner's place—and of

116

reparation—of the ram somehow compensating God for the loss he suffered as a result of sin".

This is what Jesus has done once and for all. He has died in our place to bear our death sentence, and he has compensated God through his perfect life offered up to death.

Just how deep is the love of God? We would never know were it not for the cross. We would be like those miners looking down into the darkness, not knowing how deep the lake was. But the cross is like the weighted line by which we gauge the depths of God's love. This is God's eternal plan. The Son of God would plumb the depths of sin and hell in our place. And all the world would see just how far his love goes. We would look on and cry, "Worthy is the Lamb".

How far does God's love go? All the way down.

Meditate

Very rarely will anyone die for a righteous person,
though for a good person someone might possibly
dare to die.
But God demonstrates his own love for us in this:
while we were still sinners, Christ died for us.

Romans 5 v 7-8

This is love:
not that we loved God,
but that he loved us
and sent his Son as an atoning sacrifice for our sins.

1 John 4 v 10

TUESDAY

And though the LORD makes his life an offering for sin,
he will see his offspring and prolong his days,
and the will of the LORD will prosper in his hand.
(Isaiah 53 v 10)

I have a few interesting facts to share with anyone who will listen. Did you know, for example, that pink used to be a boys' colour? Among those who will *not* listen—not anymore—are my daughters. They've heard them all before. They greet all my wonderful tidbits of information with a groan. I wonder what topic *you're* known for going on about?

This section of Isaiah's song is made up of three pairs. There are:

- *two references to "the LORD's will" in verse 10;*
- *two descriptions of the servant sharing his victory: he will justify many in verse 11 and share the spoils in verse 12;*
- *two references to Jesus' connection to "transgressors" in verse 12.*

Here's the first pair: Isaiah says it was *the Lord's will* to crush Jesus the Servant; then he says it's *the Lord's will* to prosper Jesus the Servant (v 10).

The word "though" is better translated "if" or "when". The idea is, "*If and when* the LORD makes [the servant's] life an offering for sin, *then* … he will prolong his days." "Life" here is not life as opposed to death but life "poured out … unto death" (v 12). When God treats the servant's death as a satisfactory guilt offering, then God will raise the servant from the dead.

Flip this idea round: see it fulfilled in Jesus, and it becomes a powerful confirmation of our salvation. If God has raised Jesus from the dead, then God has accepted his death as a guilt offering. And God *has* raised Jesus from the dead! Our guilt has been covered. Reparation has been made. Compensation has been provided. All the demands of God's holy law have been satisfied. The proof is the empty tomb.

Whenever you feel the weight of your sin, whenever you feel the nagging pain of guilt, whenever you doubt God's love for you—you can look at the cross for there is God's love on display. But you can also look at the empty tomb. That's the sign that God has accepted Christ's offering and therefore God has accepted *you*.

Not only does Jesus atone for our sin; he lives again to see the fruit of his suffering. "He will see his offspring and prolong his days." Every other lord will one day die, never to rise again (Isaiah 26 v 13-14). But the days of Jesus will continue for ever. In 25 v 6-8, Isaiah describes a wonderful feast. It's an evocative picture of a banquet at the end of time when we will eat with God. But the striking thing about this feast is that death itself is on the menu: "he will swallow up death for ever" (v 8).

Jesus will live to see his "offspring". These are not physical offspring birthed from a mother, but spiritual offspring birthed by the Holy Spirit. Jesus will rise again to see new life come to his people. God has accepted the cross as an offering for sin, and the proof is the empty tomb; and so every day new people are being born again as children of God.

There would be no Christians and there would be no church were it not for the cross. And there will be no new Christians and no church growth except through the preaching of the cross. That's why Paul says he was determined to preach nothing "except Jesus Christ and him crucified" (1 Corinthians 2 v 2). That's why the cross must be at the centre of our outreach.

People should never encounter you or your church for long without noticing that you go on about the cross a lot! What would it take, and what would need to change, for people to notice that about *you*?

Meditate

"Where, O death, is your victory?
Where, O death, is your sting?"

The sting of death is sin,
and the power of sin is the law.
But thanks be to God!
He gives us the victory through our Lord Jesus Christ.
Therefore, my dear brothers and sisters, stand firm.
Let nothing move you.
Always give yourselves fully to the work of the Lord,
because you know that your labour in the Lord
is not in vain.

1 Corinthians 15 v 55-58

WEDNESDAY

After he has suffered,
he will see the light of life and be satisfied;
by his knowledge my righteous servant will justify many,
and he will bear their iniquities.
(Isaiah 53 v 11)

I'm sure you know the pleasure of a job well done: the clean kitchen, the empty in-tray, the mended shirt, the completed project, the erected shelves. Jesus had a job to do: saving his people. What pleasure will there be for him in a job well done?

There was no pleasure in his suffering. The NIV translation of verse 11—"After he has suffered"—is a bit tame. It's literally "because of the suffering or anguish of his soul". This is a suffering that penetrates to the deepest part of his being. It's the word used of a woman in labour, struggling to give birth to her offspring. Here we discover the labour pains through which people are born again as God's children.

Consider for a moment the words Isaiah has used to describe the suffering of the servant: *appalling, disfigured, marred, despised, rejected, suffering, pain, punished, stricken, afflicted, pierced, crushed, wounded, oppressed, cut off.* Now let's add in all the negative statements: *the servant is beyond human likeness, has no beauty, has no majesty, has nothing desirable, is held in low esteem.* Feel the cumulative force of these descriptions. This is Christ's love for you. He suffered in this way for you.

He has suffered, but now he is satisfied. "For the joy that was set before him," says Hebrews 12 v 2, "he endured the cross, scorning its shame". The cross was not an empty gesture. It had a purpose, and that purpose was joy. And the joy for which Jesus suffered is *you*! He died for his people, and now he lives to see his offspring (Isaiah 53 v 10). If you've put your faith in Christ, then you've been redeemed from sin and reconciled to God. And Jesus is happy with what he sees. Your salvation is his satisfaction. When he looks at you, he is pleased with what he sees. He look at you and says, *It was worth it.*

Pause for a moment and think about that.

It's not clear whether "by his knowledge" in 53 v 11 means "through his know-how" or "by knowing him". It could mean that Jesus the Servant knew what was required and acted on that knowledge to save his people (using the wisdom described in 52 v 13). Or it could mean that the servant reveals the way back to God. But the focus in this section is not on the servant as prophet but on the servant as saviour. So it's more likely to mean that by knowing the servant—by us putting our faith in him—he justifies many.

The word "justify" means "make righteous" or "make right" with God. It's the same word used to describe the servant: the *righteous* servant makes us *righteous*. The servant was condemned by humanity. "We considered him punished by God" (53 v 4). But God has vindicated him by raising him from the dead. His resurrection is God's declaration that his Servant was in the right all along.

But the amazing thing is that Jesus the Servant shares his vindication with us. He is righteous, and now we are righteous in him. How can he do this when in fact we're clearly in the wrong? Because, as Isaiah continues, "he will bear their iniquities" (v 11). At the cross, Jesus took away our sin and the penalty it deserves. Then through his resurrection, he justified us in God's sight. Paul must surely have had Isaiah 53 in mind when he wrote, "He was delivered over to death for our sins and was raised to life for our justification" (Romans 4 v 25).

The resurrection turned the world's verdict upside down: the condemnation of Jesus by the world became vindication by God. But those who are in Christ get turned upside down in the process. The condemned become the justified. Sinners are declared righteous. And Jesus is satisfied.

Meditate

Your faith will be established,
and your hearts comforted,
when you have come to Christ.
For the more fully the suffering of Christ,
which is the object of your faith,
is spread before your eyes,
the more your faith will be raised and established.

For if Christ suffered such great things for you,
even the very wrath of God and torments of hell,
then you may be assured that he will never forget you.

Can a woman forget her child? No.
Why not? Because she suffered to give it birth.
But look, here is a suffering beyond all sufferings:
Christ suffering
in the greatness of his love for poor sinners,
suffering under the wrath of God his Father.
How can he forget you who are his offspring?

William Bridge (c. 1600-1670)

THURSDAY

Therefore I will give him a portion among the great,
and he will divide the spoils with the strong.
(Isaiah 53 v 12)

I wonder if you feel fragile. You may feel emotionally fragile, as if you might fall apart at any moment. Or your church might feel fragile, so that you wonder if you'll be able to continue if another family leaves. Or maybe there are times when your salvation seems fragile. You're not so much a saint marching into battle as a wounded soldier limping home.

Jesus shares his vindication, as we have seen. And he also shares his victory. The word "great" is a bit misleading. While it can mean "great", it can also mean "many" or "numerous" (Exodus 1 v 7), and that's what it means throughout this song. This is crucial to the *poetry* of the song. For the word "many" is repeated at the end of Isaiah 53 v 12 ("he bore the sin of many"). So there's a double "many" at the end of the song which echoes the double "many" at the beginning of the song (52 v 14-15).

But it's also crucial to the *message* of the song. It's not that the servant is cosying up to the great and the good. The "many" are "his offspring" in 53 v 10, and those whom he "justified" in verse 11. Henri Blocher says, "The concluding promise of the Song, therefore, is not that the Servant will be promoted to the ranks of the great captains and mighty warriors. The promise is that he will share the riches he has obtained by his victory with a multitude of needy [people], for whom he freely consented to die."

Jesus himself echoes the "many" of Isaiah 53 when he says in Matthew 20 v 28, "The Son of Man did not come to be served, but to serve, and to give his life as a ransom for many". *We* are the many. This is us. This is you if you've put your faith in Christ.

It also helps to realise that the words "give", "portion" and "divide" are all the same word in Hebrew. Put this all together, and we get this more literal translation of this verse:

> *Therefore I will allocate many as an allocation to him*
> *and he will allocate the strong as plunder.*

God does the allocating in the first line: he gives many people to the servant. The servant does the allocating in the second line: he invites us to share in his victory.

Do you remember how this song started? "He will sprinkle many nations, and kings will shut their mouths because of him" (52 v 15). We find the same idea again. Isaiah begins and ends his song with the same note. At the beginning the servant *cleanses* many; here (53 v 11) the servant *justifies* many. At the beginning the world falls silent as the servant is vindicated; at the end the world is defeated and the strong are allocated as plunder.

What's the servant's reward? Us. You and I. God's people. The church. And he is satisfied.

What's our reward? At the moment we're besieged and beset by the world around. In the West we're mocked and marginalised. Elsewhere in the world Christians are persecuted and imprisoned. But the strong don't win. *We win!* In fact, we've already won—for Jesus has risen from the dead. They did their worst and it was not enough to overcome Jesus. They can do their worst to us, but nothing will separate us from the love of God in Christ Jesus.

Meditate

Crown him with many crowns,
The Lamb upon his throne.
Hark! How the heavenly anthem drowns
All music but its own.
Awake, my soul, and sing of him who died for thee,
And hail him as thy matchless King through all eternity.

Crown him the Lord of life,
Who triumphed over the grave,

And rose victorious in the strife
For those he came to save.
His glories now we sing, who died, and rose on high,
Who died eternal life to bring, and lives that death may die.

Crown him the Lord of love,
Behold his hands and side,
Those wounds, yet visible above,
In beauty glorified.
No angel in the sky can fully bear that sight,
But downward bends his burning eye at mysteries so bright.

Matthew Bridges (1800-1894)

FRIDAY

Because he poured out his life unto death,
and was numbered with the transgressors.
(Isaiah 53 v 12)

Jesus has received the victory. He is like an athlete receiving the gold medal, a conqueror receiving the plunder, a hero being honoured. Why does Jesus deserve this reward? "Because he poured out his life unto death, and was numbered with the transgressors" (v 12).

Again Isaiah reminds us that Jesus died willingly. His life was not taken from him against his will. He poured it out. And again Isaiah reminds us that he died in our place. On the night before he died, Jesus quoted verse 12: "It is written: 'And he was numbered with the transgressors'; and I tell you that this must be fulfilled in me. Yes, what is written about me is reaching its fulfilment" (Luke 22 v 37). That would be graphically fulfilled the next day as he hung between two criminals: one, two, three criminals crucified in a line.

But that picture points to a deeper meaning and a deeper fulfilment: Jesus aligns himself with transgressors. He stands with us—with you, with me—that we might stand with him. "God made him who had no sin to be sin for us, so that in him we might become the righteousness of God" (2 Corinthians 5 v 21).

The Puritan John Flavel imagines the Father and Son in conversation as they agree the plan of salvation.

The Father:
My Son, here is a company of poor miserable souls that have utterly undone themselves, and now lie open to my justice! Justice demands satisfaction for them, or it will satisfy itself in their eternal ruin. What shall be done for these souls?

The Son:
O my Father, such is my love towards them, and my pity for them, that I will be responsible for them rather than see them perish eternally. I will be their Guarantor. Bring in all your bills, that I may see what they owe you. Lord, bring them all in, that there may be nothing left. From my hand you shall receive all you require. I will choose to suffer your wrath rather than allow them to suffer it. Upon me, my Father, upon me be all their debt.

The Father:
But, my Son, if you undertake for them, you must reckon to pay the last penny. Expect no mitigation. If I spare them, then I will not spare you.

The Son:
I am content with this, Father. Let it be so. Charge it all to me. I am able to pay it in full. And though it prove my undoing, though it impoverish all my riches and empty all my treasures (for so indeed it did as 2 Corinthians 8 v 9 says, "Though he was rich, yet for our sakes he became poor"), yet I am content to undertake it.

Flavel concludes by addressing himself to professing Christians who are reluctant to obey Christ:

Blush, ungrateful believers. Let shame cover your faces. Judge in yourselves: has Christ deserved that you should argue about trifles, that you should shrink from a few petty difficulties, and complain that this is hard or harsh? Oh, if you knew the grace of our Lord Jesus Christ in this, his wonderful condescension for you, you could not do it.

Meditate
*What our Lord wants us to present to him
is not goodness, nor honesty, nor endeavour,
but real, solid sin: that is all he can take from us.
And what does he give in exchange for our sin?
Real, solid righteousness.*

Oswald Chambers (1874-1917)

SATURDAY

For he bore the sin of many,
and made intercession for the transgressors.
(Isaiah 53 v 12)

Have you ever let your mind wander only to be caught out? It happens to me all the time. The topic of conversation and the topic in my inner thought-world head off in different directions. Then someone asks me a question and I've got no idea what people have been talking about. What is it, do you think, that's on Jesus' mind at this present moment?

Jesus not only aligns himself with transgressors; he also intercedes for them. In Luke's account of the crucifixion we read, "When they came to the place called the Skull, they crucified him there, along with the criminals—one on his right, the other on his left. Jesus said, 'Father, forgive them, for they do not know what they are doing'" (Luke 23 v 33-34).

It's one thing to forgive those who've caused us pain. That's difficult, but it happens. It's quite another thing to do so as that pain is being inflicted. Yet this is what Jesus did. As the nails were driven into his flesh, Jesus thought not of himself but of his torturers. He prayed to the Father on their behalf.

The reference to "many" in today's verse brings us back to where we started, both in this verse ("I will give him a portion among the great" or "*many*") and in the song as a whole ("Just as there were *many* who were appalled at him ... so he will sprinkle *many* nations" in 52 v 14-15). That moment of intercession was a sign of a life and death and life again of intercession for the many who are his.

Life. Throughout his life, Jesus interceded on behalf of his disciples. "During the days of his life on earth," says Hebrews 5 v 7, Jesus "offered up prayers and petitions with fervent cries and tears". It was this intercession that saved Simon Peter from ruin. Even as Jesus predicted that Peter would deny him, he also said, "I have prayed for you, Simon, that your faith may not fail" (Luke 22 v 32).

Death. Through his death, Jesus interceded for his people. "He bore the sin of many." He placed himself between us and God's judgment. The basis of Christ's intercession is his finished work on the cross. And his work on the cross is constantly applied by his intercession.

Life eternal. "Now there have been many of those priests, since death prevented them from continuing in office," says Hebrews 7 v 23-25, "but because Jesus lives for ever, he has a permanent priesthood. Therefore he is able to save completely those who come to God through him, because he always lives to intercede for them." The *intercession* of Jesus never ends because the *priesthood* of

Jesus never ends. He lives for ever, and he lives for ever to secure our place in heaven. He is there before the Father as the permanent reminder of his finished work. Our place in heaven is as secure as that of Jesus himself.

Jesus lights up heaven with his glory. He sits at the Father's right hand, for his sufferings are complete. The victory he has secured and the price he has paid are the wonder of heaven. Angelic choirs sing his praise while he reigns above all powers and beyond all danger.

And what's he thinking about? What's on his mind? You and me. "How can we hear without amazement," asks Charles Spurgeon, "that his heart steals away from all heaven's joys to remember such poor creatures as we are and make incessant prayer on our behalf?"

It's as if Jesus constantly slips away from the heavenly party held in his honour to ensure we are safe and secure.

Meditate

It's time to make Isaiah's song your own. I've changed the pronouns so it talks explicitly about Jesus and about you (the changes are in italics). Read it through slowly, lingering on each line, as an expression of faith in Jesus the Servant and his death on your behalf.

> Surely *Jesus* took up *my* pain
> and bore *my* suffering,
> yet *I* considered *Jesus* punished by God,
> stricken by him, and afflicted.

But *Jesus* was pierced for *my* transgressions,
Jesus was crushed for *my* iniquities;
the punishment that brought *me* peace was on *Jesus*,
and by the wounds of *Jesus I am* healed.
I, like a sheep, have gone astray,
I have turned to *my* own way;
and the LORD has laid on *Jesus my* iniquity.

Because Jesus has suffered,
he will see the light of life and be satisfied;
when people know *Jesus*, God's righteous servant,
Jesus will justify many,
and *Jesus* will bear *our* iniquities.
Therefore *the* LORD *will allocate many people
as a reward to Jesus,*
and *Jesus will allocate the strong as plunder to his people,*
because *Jesus* poured out his life unto death,
and was numbered with the transgressors.
For *Jesus* bore the sin of many *including me*,
and made intercession for the transgressors *like me*.

HOLY WEEK & EASTER SUNDAY

The
Invitation

PALM SUNDAY

Isaiah 54 – 55

8 th May 1945. VE Day. "Victory in Europe" at the end of the Second World War. Crowds spontaneously spilled out onto the streets. People embraced strangers in joy. Church bells rang out. Flags were waved. Songs were sung. The war had been won and so the celebrations began.

Isaiah 53 ended with the victory of Jesus the Servant. Now it's time to celebrate. Isaiah's very next words are an exhortation to sing: "Sing, barren woman" (54 v 1). Isaiah 54 and 55 describe the blessings that flow from the death and resurrection of Jesus. *We're* the barren woman. She represents the people of God. Left to ourselves, we're unable to produce any offspring. But the Lord has promised that the servant "will see his offspring" (53 v 10). The death of Jesus brings life to the children of God. And so we have plenty of reasons to sing.

Indeed, it's not just God's people who sing. Today is Palm Sunday. As Jesus was entering Jerusalem, some of the Pharisees called on him to quieten the people. Jesus replied, "If they keep quiet, the stones will cry out" (Luke 19 v 40). Perhaps Jesus had Isaiah 55 v 12 in mind: "the mountains and hills will burst into song before you". The whole of creation bursts into song because the resurrection of Jesus is the beginning of the renewal of all things.

As you read chapters 54 – 55, look out for the commands. They come thick and fast. Yet not one of them is onerous: "Shout for joy." "Do not be afraid." "Eat what is good." God is urging us to share the victory that Jesus the Servant has won.

Pray
Pray through the reading by taking a verse or two at a time. Each time identify…
• something to praise God for
• something to confess
• something to turn into a request

MONDAY

Isaiah 54 v 1-3
Sing barren woman … Enlarge the place of your tent.

Imagine waking up one day and finding you have a house full of children, and they're complaining that the house is too small! Where have they all come from?! Surely you would have remembered if you'd given birth to dozens of children. Yet this is what Isaiah says will happen to God's people:

Though you were ruined and made desolate
and your land laid waste,
now you will be too small for your people,
and those who devoured you will be far away.
The children born during your bereavement
will yet say in your hearing,
"This place is too small for us;
give us more space to live in."
Then you will say in your heart,
"Who bore me these?
I was bereaved and barren;
I was exiled and rejected.
Who brought these up?
I was left all alone,
but these—where have they come from?"
(Isaiah 49 v 19-21)

The people of Israel will look at the people of God and say, *I don't remember giving birth to all these children!* But, of course, these children are not all ethnic Jews. The nations have come and joined God's people. They have swelled the number beyond measure.

God says to Jesus the Servant, "It is too small a thing for you to be my servant to restore the tribes of Jacob" (49 v 6). The cross deserves more than just the people from one nation, as we saw on Ash Wednesday (p 10). So God continues, "I will also make you a light for the Gentiles, that my salvation may reach to the ends of the earth" (v 6).

But this creates a problem. Lots of people are being gathered into the family of God and there's nowhere to put them all! In 49 v 20 what's "too small" is the place for us all to live in. It's as if we're all crammed into a small area of land on the eastern edge of the Mediterranean, and people are saying, "This place is never going to be big enough. We need a new heaven and a new earth." And soon Isaiah will tell us that's exactly what's coming (65 v 17).

Isaiah repeats this idea in 54 v 1-3. The word "offspring" in 53 v 10 is the same as the word "descendants" in 54 v 3. The servant died to see his offspring and justify many (53 v 10-11). As a result, it's time to enlarge the tent so there's room to fit them all in. God's people are like a barren woman who now has a vast brood of children. So it's time to build an extension (54 v 2).

The story of salvation had started with a barren woman—Sarah, the wife of Abraham. She had borne a child in her old age, and so the story continued when it looked as if it might fail. Now, as the story reaches its climax, the barren woman is God's people as a whole rejoicing to see many new children.

The church in the West feels small. We see few conversions. Numbers are declining. Churches are closing. But remember, this is just one place in the world and this is just one moment in history. A day is coming when we will say, as the people do in 49 v 21, *"I was left alone, but these—where have they come from?"*

One day we will stand around the throne of the Lamb and see people stretching as far as the eye can see. And we will say, *"Where have they have all come from?"* And then maybe we will say, "Worthy is the Lamb. This is the reward that Christ deserves."

Meditate

You are worthy to take the scroll
and to open its seals,
because you were slain,
and with your blood you purchased for God
persons from every tribe and language
and people and nation.
You have made them to be a kingdom and priests
to serve our God,
and they will reign on the earth.

Revelation 5 v 9-10

TUESDAY

Isaiah 54 v 4-8
Do not fear disgrace; you will not be humiliated.

When my friend got divorced, she stopped going out. Even though she was the innocent party, she felt the shame of being a once-married woman. Plus at the kind of dinner parties she frequented, people didn't really know what to do with a divorcee. Everything was built around couples. Perhaps you've seen that or felt that too.

Or consider the question: why have you never had children? However it's intended, it's hard not to hear it as an accusation. Subtext: what have you got against children?

Sadly, being childless or divorced can be a source of shame. The very word "childless" defines someone in terms of what they lack. In Isaiah 54, God's people are likened to a barren woman (v 1) and then a rejected wife (v 6). In this relationship, there is no question who is guilty: Israel has been an unfaithful wife and so God has abandoned her to her adulteries. The result is desolation, fear, shame, disgrace, humiliation, reproach and distress (v 1, 4, 6).

But all that is about to change.

Jesus was disfigured so we can be made beautiful. Humanity was made in the image of God to reflect his glory. We were beautiful because we reflected the beauty of God. But our sin marred that image. Our hearts became ugly. Even our bodies were affected: we grow sick and old.

On the cross, Jesus the Servant was disfigured beyond recognition and his form was marred (52 v 14). He became un-beautiful. But "by his wounds we are healed" (53 v 5). Through his disfigurement we are made "beautiful and glorious" (4 v 2). As a result, our shame and reproach are removed (54 v 4). In 61 v 1-3, Jesus himself speaks:

> *The Spirit of the Sovereign* LORD *is on me …*
> *to comfort all who mourn, and provide for those who*
> *grieve in Zion—*
> *to bestow on them a crown of beauty instead of ashes,*
> *the oil of joy instead of mourning,*
> *and a garment of praise instead of a spirit of despair.*

Jesus was abandoned so we can be welcomed back. As he died, Jesus cried, "My God, why have your forsaken me?"

(Mark 15 v 34). On the cross, God unleashed "a surge of anger" against sin, hiding his face as darkness covered the land (Isaiah 54 v 8). Now, as a result, "the LORD will call you back" (v 6). Jesus is reclaiming his bride.

Imagine a bride turning up for her wedding looking filthy and dishevelled because she's been rolling in the mud with her lovers. Her husband-to-be turns away and she is left to face the disgrace she has brought on herself. Except that this husband returns with a set of beautiful new clothes which he has bought at great personal cost. "Christ loved the church and gave himself up for her," says Ephesians 5 v 25-27, "to make her holy, cleansing her by the washing with water through the word, and to present her to himself as a radiant church, without stain or wrinkle or any other blemish, but holy and blameless". God gives his people a new name: "Hephzibah" (62 v 4). It means "my delight is in her".

Isaiah is addressing God's people as a whole here. But there's also an important message here to those who are single, divorced or childless. Jesus says, "Do not be afraid; you will not be put to shame. Do not fear disgrace; you will not be humiliated ... with everlasting kindness, I will have compassion on you" (54 v 4, 8).

"As a bridegroom rejoices over his bride, so will your God rejoice over you" (61 v 5). If you can embrace that promise, then you will be an important sign within the Christian community that ultimate fulfilment is not found in human marriage or families. Fulfilment is found in our relationship with Christ.

Meditate

I delight greatly in the LORD;
my soul rejoices in my God.
For he has clothed me with garments of salvation
and arrayed me in a robe of his righteousness,
as a bridegroom adorns his head like a priest,
and as a bride adorns herself with her jewels.

Isaiah 61 v 10

WEDNESDAY

Isaiah 54 v 9-10
My unfailing love for you will not be shaken.

All this talk of Christ paying the penalty of our sin and reclaiming his bride is all well and good. But can it last? What's to stop humanity rejecting God and God responding in judgment all over again? Just how secure is the future Christ has won for his people?

To help us look forward with confidence, God first invites us to look back. "To me this is like the days of Noah," says God in verse 9, "when I swore that the waters of Noah would never again cover the earth". In the first generations after Adam's sin, humanity declined until "every inclination of the thoughts of the human heart was only evil all the time" (Genesis 6 v 5). So

God sent a flood to wipe out humanity. Only Noah and his family were saved (along with two of each kind of animal) so that humanity could start again.

When the floods waters had finally subsided and Noah stepped from the ark, God made this promise: "I establish my covenant with you: never again will all life be destroyed by the waters of a flood; never again will there be a flood to destroy the earth" (Genesis 9 v 11). Isaiah echoes the words "never again" in 54 v 9. God can make these promises because he has a permanent solution to humanity's sin in mind. That solution is *Jesus*.

So this moment is replicated. Just as Noah stepped out of the ark, so Jesus steps from the tomb. God again promises, "Never again". Only this time it's not simply "never again will there be a flood". This time, God says he will never again be angry with his people (v 9).

There are three reasons for this "never again".

First, Jesus has paid the penalty of sin in full. God can say, "Never again" because Jesus has said, "It is finished" (John 19 v 30). God's anger is "never again" because it's no more. There's nothing left. God's anger is not a mood that might return. It's not an emotion that might spin out of control. It's his settled opposition to evil and his determination to see justice done. And now for God's people, justice *has* been done—in full at the cross.

Second, just as God has never again flooded the earth, as he promised in his covenant with Noah (Isaiah 54 v 9), so now he promises in an eternal covenant of peace never again to judge his people.

Though the mountains be shaken
and the hills be removed,
yet my unfailing love for you will not be shaken
nor my covenant of peace be removed.

(v 10; see also 66 v 22)

Third, we will see the glory and grace of God as never before. At the moment, we see only by faith and we keep getting distracted. But one day "we shall be like him, for we shall see him as he is" (1 John 3 v 2). Never again will sin seem appealing. Isn't that wonderful?

The cross reveals not only the depths of divine love but also the depths of human sin. Temptation always presents sin as attractive. But the cross unmasks sin. At the cross, we see sin in its true colours. This is what our sin is really like: when we get the chance, we murder our Creator. And this is where our sin leads: as Jesus bore our sin, he was ruined.

The unspiritual eye looks at the cross and turns away from Jesus (Isaiah 53 v 3). The spiritual eye looks at the cross and turns away from sin.

Meditate

Sin is not as sweet as the sinner imagines.
Christ suffered bitter things when he bore it in his body
upon the tree.
Sin lies when it flatters you with hopes of some contentment.
Sin always smiles upon the soul when it first comes.
But remember it cost Christ dearly.
Sin is a flattering, deceiving thing.

Thomas Manton (1620-1677)

THURSDAY

Isaiah 54 v 11-17
No weapon forged against you will prevail.

"**A**fflicted city, lashed by storms and not comforted." I wonder if that captures how you feel at this moment in time. Perhaps it's external troubles that assail you—a job loss, a bereavement, an illness, some conflict. Perhaps it's internal doubts or the black dog of depression or a lack of assurance.

In verses 4-10, God promises that he will "never again" be angry with his people. But God is not our only threat. What about all the problems we face? We live in a dangerous world; we face a hostile culture; we battle with a satanic enemy. Yet we need not fear, for God becomes a builder and blacksmith to protect his people (v 11, 16).

- *God will restore the splendour of his people (v 11-12).*
- *God himself will teach his people (v 13).*
- *God will remove tyranny from his people (v 14).*
- *God will thwart anyone who tries to attack his people (v 15-16).*
- *God will grant his people vindication—literally "righteousness" (v 17).*

They're beautiful promises and I want to encourage you to make them your own.

We sometimes talk about someone "going to pieces" or "falling apart". We reach a point of emotional disintegration.

But God promises, "I will rebuild ... all your walls of precious stones" (v 11-12).

Perhaps you feel unsettled. It may be a vague sense of unease; it may be full-on panic attacks. Your life is full of fears. Your world feels out of control.

But God promises, "Great will be their peace ... Terror will be far removed" (v 13-14).

Perhaps you face hostility in your home from unbelieving relatives. Or perhaps you face hostility in the workplace. People mock your faith. They ask questions you can't answer. They taunt you with the failings of the wider church.

But God promises, "You will refute every tongue that accuses you" (v 17).

All of these promises we can experience in some measure in this life. But all of them will find their ultimate fulfilment when Christ returns. "This is the heritage of the servants of the LORD" (v 17). And one day that inheritance will be yours.

There's one more thing to notice in these verses. Isaiah has talked a lot about the servant of the Lord and all that he will achieve. But here for the first time, he talks about "the servants [plural] of the LORD" (v 17). The nation of Israel was supposed to be a light to the nations, making God known in the world. But she failed and ended up in exile. And so God promised another Servant: Jesus. But through Jesus, the people of God are rebooted. We are reborn as God's people. Who is the servant of the Lord in the world? *You and your church.*

Meditate

We have a strong city;
God makes salvation its walls and ramparts.
Open the gates that the righteous nation may enter,
the nation that keeps faith.
You will keep in perfect peace
those whose minds are steadfast,
because they trust in you.
Trust in the LORD for ever,
for the LORD, the LORD himself,
is the Rock eternal.

Isaiah 26 v 1-4

GOOD FRIDAY

Isaiah 55 v 1-2
Come, all you who are thirsty.

saiah has described the suffering and victory of the servant. Now he issues an invitation—*the* invitation. You'll never receive a better invitation than this. This is the invitation that flows from the work of the cross, the invitation that comes to us in the gospel.

> *Come, all you who are thirsty, come to the waters;*
> *and you who have no money, come, buy and eat!*
> *Come, buy wine and milk without money and*
> *without cost.*   *(Isaiah 55 v 1)*

"Come ... come ... come ... come." Four times. Isaiah is like a street-seller raising his voice above the crowd. That's because there's lots of "noise" about. The world is full of other propositions, all clamouring for our attention. Every advert we see promises satisfaction. But this is a promise of *eternal* satisfaction.

This invitation goes to all nations (v 5). Yet so many people turn away. We opt for alternatives. We seek fulfilment in sex, career, possessions, health, relationships. They're all good things. But they make poor substitutes for God.

> *Why spend money on what is not bread,*
> *and your labour on what does not satisfy?*
> *Listen, listen to me, and eat what is good,*
> *and you will delight in the richest of fare.*
>   *(Isaiah 55 v 2)*

These alternatives offer poor returns. If you look for fulfilment in anything apart from God, then you'll find it "does not satisfy". While it's just beyond your reach, you might imagine it giving lasting pleasure. But if ever you attain your goal, you'll find yourself disappointed. Unless that goal is God himself.

And these alternatives demand a high price. If you live for career, then you may find yourself sacrificing relationships. If you live to win, then you must sacrifice many hours for training. If you live for acceptance, then you must constantly be evaluating how you've been evaluated by others. It's exhausting.

What about God? What does God require? Only that you *come*. You need bring nothing with you. Just come. What's offered is beyond price; yet no price is demanded. The price tag reads, "Without cost" (v 1). It's not that there isn't a price. But the price has been paid. It was paid with the shed blood of the Son of God. In John's account of Good Friday, we read, "Knowing that everything had now been finished, and so that Scripture would be fulfilled, Jesus said, 'I am thirsty'" (John 19 v 28). Jesus was thirsty so that he could say to us, "Come, all you who are thirsty" (Isaiah 55 v 1; John 4 v 14).

If today you're weary, dry, troubled, empty or frustrated, then come to Jesus. It doesn't matter whether you're coming for the first time or the hundredth time. "Come, all you who are thirsty, come to the waters."

Meditate

The gospel is so precious a thing that,
if it is to be bought,
the whole world could not pay for it.
And therefore if bought at all, it must be without
money and without price!

It cost the Lord Jesus his blood—
what have you to offer?
What? Do you imagine that you can buy it with
a few paltry works?
God himself must become a man and bleed and die
to bring pardon and eternal life to sinners!
And do you think that your tears, bending your knees,
gifts of money, and emotions of your heart
can purchase this unpurchasable blessing?
Oh, believe, because it is so rich,
it must be given away if it is to belong to us!

C. H. Spurgeon (1834-1892)

SATURDAY

Isaiah 55 v 3-11
Seek the LORD while he may be found.

Holy Saturday is a strange time in the liturgical calendar. We find ourselves in a kind of twilight zone between the darkness of Good Friday and the sunshine of Easter Sunday. Between sorrow and joy. Between death and life.

And yet Holy Saturday is where we live our lives. We live between the cross and resurrection. The resurrection of Jesus is the beginning and promise of a new era.

Jesus has gone ahead of us. But we're not there yet. For us, resurrection is a future reality. In the meantime, we live in an age still marked by the cross. It's a world still experiencing suffering and decay. We ourselves take up our cross each day as we follow Jesus. For us, the glory of the resurrection is still to come.

This "pause" in the story of salvation is a divine gift. We might well wish God would hasten the day when Easter Sunday dawns as a universal experience. But God is patient. This Saturday-era is given that people might turn to him in repentance. It's a time of mercy before Christ returns to judge the living and the dead.

Isaiah anticipates this in 55 v 3-11 with three lovely promises.

1. The nations will run home to God (v 3-5). It can be a bit tricky trying to work who Isaiah is talking about in these verses, until you remember that the nation of Israel had failed as God's servant to draw the nations to God; but now Jesus has fulfilled this role and transformed God's people. So Isaiah is saying that *Jesus* will make God known to the nations ("I have made him a witness to the peoples", v 4). But Isaiah is also saying that through Jesus, *God's people* will make God known to the nations ("you will summon nations you know not", v 5). So this is a promise to us if we're in Christ: "Nations you do not know will come running to you". This promise is being fulfilled across the world this very day through the mission of the church.

2. God is near and ready to show mercy (v 6-7). These verses are first and foremost an exhortation to turn to God.

But they contain implicit and explicit promises: *God may be found; God is near; God will show mercy; God will freely pardon.* "How gracious he will be when you cry for help! As soon as he hears, he will answer you" (30 v 19).

But there is also an implicit threat. We're to seek the Lord "while he may be found". A time is coming when God can no longer be found. For some, this moment comes when they die; for others, it will come when Christ returns. We live in the "Saturday" of human history. It's a moment of mercy which will one day give way to the Sunday of eternity.

3. God's word will always bear fruit (55 v 8-11). I sometimes think I would do a better job of running the world than God. Of course, I don't say it like that—I'm not a complete idiot. But every time I complain about what's happening in my life, that's what I'm implying. But, says God, *my thoughts are higher than your thoughts* (v 9). It's God's gentle way of reminding us that we don't really know what's going on. We're not well equipped to make judgments about the course of human affairs. Our notions of who God is and our plans for saving ourselves are turned upside down when we stand before the cross. We're to turn from our own *ways* and *thoughts* in verse 7 to God's *thoughts* and *ways* in verse 8.

In contrast to our thoughts, God's word is certain and sure. It doesn't just provide information; it changes the world. "It will not return to me empty, but will accomplish what I desire" (v 11). "Hang on a moment," you might be saying. "I've shared the gospel with people who've not responded." That may be true. But we need to remember that God's purposes include both salvation and judgment. Isaiah knew this because it was central to his original commission. He was told he would "make the heart of this people calloused" (6 v 10). Paul knew it too. He said, "For we are to God the pleasing aroma of Christ among those who are being saved and those who are perishing. To the one we are an aroma that brings death; to the other, an aroma that brings life" (2 Corinthians 2 v 15-16).

Whenever you speak of Christ, it is a life-and-death moment. God's word will do something. It will confirm the judgment of those reject it. But to those who accept what you say, the word brings life, eternal life. We can't predict which it will be. But we can be sure of this: it will achieve the purpose of God.

Meditate

*God has always reassured his people by making
promises in covenants.
Let these covenants reassure your heart today.*

*The covenant with Abraham means,
just as Abraham was promised a son,
so the church is promised many children. (54 v 1).*

*The covenant with Noah means,
just as Noah was promised judgment never again
through water,
so the church is promised judgment never again
in any form. (54 v 9)*

The covenant with David means,
just as David was promised everlasting love,
so the church is promised everlasting love. (55 v 3)

"Though the mountains be shaken
and the hills be removed,
yet my unfailing love for you will not be shaken
nor my covenant of peace be removed,"
says the LORD, *who has compassion on you. (54 v 10)*

EASTER SUNDAY

Isaiah 55 v 12-13
The mountains and hills will burst into song.

When Adam rebelled against God, it wasn't just humanity that felt the effects. Adam was told:

Cursed is the ground because of you;
through painful toil you will eat food from it
all the days of your life.
It will produce thorns and thistles for you,
and you will eat the plants of the field.
(Genesis 3 v 17-18)

But Jesus the Servant is the second Adam. Unlike the first Adam, Jesus has proved himself faithful to God in life and in death. And so through his obedience, the curse gives way to blessing.

That's what Isaiah means when he says, "Instead of the thorn-bush will grow the juniper". It's not that Isaiah has a dislike of hawthorn blossom. In this verse, thorns represent the intrusion of evil and decay into God's good world. But the day is coming when the curse will be reversed and creation made new.

That day is Easter Sunday. At least, that's when the renewal of creation began. Jesus rose from the dead, leaving death behind. And his resurrection was not just an individual act that affected his body. His resurrection was a corporate act that forever changed the future of God's people. It was a re-creative act—the beginning of the renewal of all things. Jesus is the second Adam: the beginning of a new humanity and the beginning of the lifting of the curse.

Paul says, "The creation was subjected to frustration" and "the whole creation has been groaning as in the pains of childbirth right up to the present time" (Romans 8 v 20-22). It's Paul's vivid way of saying creation was cursed. It's as if creation is a person groaning in frustration—like you do perhaps when you feel your aches and pains or when you've had a bad day.

But one day "the creation itself will be liberated from its bondage to decay and brought into the freedom and glory of the children of God" (8 v 21). On that day it will stop groaning. What will it do instead? Isaiah tells us: "The mountains and hills will burst into song before you, and all the trees of the field will clap their hands" (Isaiah 55 v 12). It's Isaiah's way of expressing the wonder of a renewed creation. Eden will be restored.

The LORD will surely comfort Zion
  and will look with compassion on all her ruins;
he will make her deserts like Eden,
  her wastelands like the garden of the LORD.
Joy and gladness will be found in her,
  thanksgiving and the sound of singing. (51 v 3)

Easter Sunday is the beginning of the renewal of all things. Today you might be groaning, just like creation. But the Sunday of eternity is coming. God is going to renew all things. "The sound of weeping and of crying will be heard [among God's people] no more" (65 v 19). If you're in Christ, the firstborn from among the dead, then "you will go out in joy and be led forth in peace" (55 v 12).

This is not merely a fanciful dream. It's already begun. It began on the first Easter Day, when Jesus walked from the tomb. Even if right now we are groaning, we can thank him for this renewal today, tomorrow and always.

Meditate

See, I will create
new heavens and a new earth.
The former things will not be remembered,
nor will they come to mind.
But be glad and rejoice for ever
in what I will create,
for I will create Jerusalem to be a delight
and its people a joy.

Isaiah 65 v 17-18

See Jesus stripped of majesty (Amazing love)
Music: Colin Webster & Phil Moore | Lyrics: Tim Chester

1. See Jesus stripped of majesty:
   He hangs disfigured on a tree,
   A man of grief, by men betrayed,
   Like one from whom we turn away.
   Led like a lamb without a sound,
   In mockery with violence crowned,
   A sacrificial offering,
   Atoning for his people's sin.

   O what amazing love,
   I bow before the cross,
   My pride reduced to dust.
   What amazing love,
   It overwhelms my soul,
   My broken life made whole.

2. See Jesus cold within the grave,
   Cut off from life, our lives to save.
   We thought that God had punished him,
   But he was pierced for Adam's sin.
   Though we like sheep have often strayed,
   Our waywardness on Christ was laid.
   To heal our wounds, he drew our pain;
   To bring us peace, he bore our shame.

   O what amazing love…

3. See Jesus once again draw breath
   And rise to claim the spoils of death.
   He sees the light of life again
   And hears his ransomed people sing.

   O what amazing love,
   Forever I will praise
   The glories of your grace.
   What amazing love,
   I offer up my life,
   A grateful sacrifice
   For your amazing love,
   Your amazing love.

Go to **www.thegoodbook.com/beauty** for a free download of the sheet music and a recording of this song, based on Isaiah 53.

This book includes quotes, poems and songs from many authors. To see details of these references, go to **www.thegoodbook.com/beauty-endnotes.pdf**

the good book
COMPANY

BIBLICAL | RELEVANT | ACCESSIBLE

At The Good Book Company, we are dedicated to helping Christians and local churches grow. We believe that God's growth process always starts with hearing clearly what he has said to us through his timeless word—the Bible.

Ever since we opened our doors in 1991, we have been striving to produce Bible-based resources that bring glory to God. We have grown to become an international provider of user-friendly resources to the Christian community, with believers of all backgrounds and denominations using our books, Bible studies, devotionals, evangelistic resources, and DVD-based courses.

We want to equip ordinary Christians to live for Christ day by day, and churches to grow in their knowledge of God, their love for one another, and the effectiveness of their outreach.

Call us for a discussion of your needs or visit one of our local websites for more information on the resources and services we provide.

Your friends at The Good Book Company

thegoodbook.com | thegoodbook.co.uk
thegoodbook.com.au | thegoodbook.co.nz